PRAISE FOR

Living The Dream:
How to Fulfill Your God-Given Purpose

"When the Lord deposits a dream into your mind and heart, He will nurture it and grow it. Karen Griffin uses the life of Joseph in showing us precisely how God works when we listen to Him and move in the direction He takes us. *Living the Dream: How to Fulfill Your God-Given Purpose* isn't just about God's purpose for the reader. By living the dream as God intends, the reader touches and impacts the people in their own life, and God's vision increases."

—Kelly Fordyce Martindale, author of *Loved by Choice: True Stories that Celebrate Adoption*, www.kellyfordycemartindale.com

"*Living the Dream* inspires us to embrace God's purpose with confidence and intention. This book highlights how patience, adversity, and diligence propel us toward the dreams and desires God places in our hearts. The Dream Notes and Dream Work of each chapter encourage us to pursue our destiny and not settle for anything less than our Father's very best for our lives."

—Lilka Finley Raphael, pharmacist, photographer, editor and author of two devotionals, *P is for Prayer* and *God and the Garden*, www.lilkaraphael.com

"In *Living the Dream*, Karen Griffin beautifully connects Joseph's story with our own, offering encouragement for those navigating loss, delay, or disappointment. This book is a practical and hope-filled resource for anyone longing to trust God's purpose in the hardest seasons."

—Jenny Leavitt, author of *Godprints*, *Creator of the Resilient Grief Recovery Courses*, and *BCMMHC Specializing in Grief, Loss, and Trauma-informed Care*, www.jennyleavitt.com, www.resilienthope.net

"Grounded in scripture and based on the lives of Bible characters as examples, the author incorporates personal testimony and aims at the heart of the reader. This interactive book rightly emphasizes the sovereignty of God the Dream-Giver and our surrendered relationship with Him and guides toward fulfilling that for which He created us."

—Rachael M. Colby, Award winning writer, editor, encourager, faith inspirer, www.TattooItOnYourHeart.com

Living The Dream:

How to Fulfill Your God-Given Purpose

Karen Griffin

Unless otherwise noted, Scripture quotations used in this book are from *The Holy Bible*, New International Version. © 1973, 1978, 1984, 2011 International Bible Society. Used by permission of Zondervan Bible Publishers.

Other Scripture references are from the following sources:
King James Version (KJV)
New King James Version (NKJV), ©1979, 1980, 1982, Thomas Nelson, Inc. *English Standard Version* ® (ESV®) © 2001 by Crossway, a publishing ministry of Good News Publishers
New American Standard (NAS), Copyright © 1960, 1962, 1963, 1968, 1971, 1972, 1973, 1975, 1977, 1995 by THE LOCKMAN FOUNDATION
New Living Translation (NLT), copyright ©1996, 2004, 2015 by Tyndale House Foundation. Used by permission of Tyndale House Publishers, Carol Stream, Illinois 60188. All rights reserved.

Copyright © 2025 Karen Griffin. All rights reserved.

Living the Dream: How to Fulfill Your God-given Purpose, Karen Griffin
Issued in electronic and paperback formats
Paperback ISBN: 979-8-9897467-5-0
E-book ISBN: 979-8-9897467-6-7
LCCN: 2025919624
First Edition

Publisher: Dressed in Love Press, LLC.
www.drkatherinehayes.com

Cover Designer: Katherine Hutchinson-Hayes
Book Interior Designer: Jenifer Jennings

Printed in the United States of America

Table of Contents

Foreword 1

Introduction 3

Chapter 1—Beginning of a Dream 7

Chapter 2—Designed For the Dream 19

Chapter 3—Discovering the Dream 29

Chapter 4— Death of a Dream 40

Chapter 5—Dream Delays 50

Chapter 6—Temptation Threatens the Dream 61

Chapter 7—Faithful to the Current Dream 72

Chapter 8—Dreams Belong to God 82

Chapter 9—Path to the Dream 93

Chapter 10—Working the Dream 103

Chapter 11—Dreams Fulfilled 113

Chapter 12—Don't Miss Your Dream 125

Chapter 13—Dreams Come True 136

Chapter 14—The Dream Expands 147

Chapter 15—Dreams Live On 157

Acknowledgements 168

Foreword

It is both a privilege and an honor to commend this work by
Karen Griffin. As an ordained minister, a retired U.S. Army Warrant
Officer, and someone who has dedicated my post-military years to
counseling and guiding others, I am deeply impressed by the courage
and bravery displayed in Living the Dream: How to Fulfill Your
God-Given Purpose.

Far too many Christians live unfulfilled and incomplete lives,
often unsure of how to fully embrace the dreams God has placed
within them. Karen Griffin confronts this reality with grace and
boldness. Through careful study and inspired reflection, she draws us
into the life of Joseph—a man whose trials, delays, and ultimate
triumphs mirror the journey many of us face as we seek to walk in
our God-given calling.

What makes this book so powerful is not only its biblical
foundation, but also its practical challenge to each believer: to align
our lives with God's eternal purposes. Karen calls us to courageously
step into the dreams He has designed for us, trusting His timing, His
process, and His faithfulness.

This is not merely a book; it is a mighty work. It serves as both
a guide and an encouragement for all who desire to live fully
according to God's purpose—rooted in truth, strengthened by faith,
and ignited by the Spirit.

I wholeheartedly recommend Living the Dream to every believer who longs to move beyond complacency into a life of purpose and fulfillment. May you, like Joseph, rise to see your God-given dream become reality.

—Anthony Kirk Hayes, Ordained Minister, Retired U.S. Army Chief Warrant Officer Four, B.S. in Psychology with an Emphasis in Life Coaching

Introduction

Do you have a dream? Is there a burning in your heart aching to be fulfilled for God?

I believe God gives each of us the desire to serve Him in unique ways. These desires form our dreams. I first became aware of God-given dreams in my mid-twenties while studying the life of Joseph and his family. As a young mother, I read the Biblical events surrounding Joseph to my children, but God was speaking to me. He tied each happening in Joseph's life clearly to events in mine. He gave understanding, instructions, and warnings as He applied the stories to my life. Through them, my dream to teach for Him expanded, and I desired to write a book — this book, based on what He taught me through Joseph's story.

Now, a few decades later, my dream is coming true. But don't think in the past several years I've been doing nothing except waiting. God has taught me and used me in many ways, some of them as unexpected as He did with Joseph. As we study the lives of Joseph and his family, I hope you'll discover how He has been working in your life. If you haven't already, I pray you will find your God-given dream and focus on following God more purposefully as He leads you toward it. If you're currently living your dream, I hope to encourage you to keep moving forward and consider helping others along their dream path.

We will begin our study before Joseph's birth because our dreams begin before we are born. Looking at his dream and its fulfillment, we will progress through Joseph's life and how God used him to minister to others. We'll connect Joseph's dream to his ancestors and descendants, learning that God works throughout the ages to accomplish His dream for all people.

In this book, 'God's dream' refers to His plan to create people for His pleasure and redeem them after sin separated them from Him. In this, we are all part of His dream. I hope you clearly see our God-given dreams are meant to fulfill His plan. When I use the term 'God-given dream,' I'm referring to His calling for each of us to participate in His plan of restoring relationships with Him and bringing people into His family. God blesses us to be part of His dream and entrusts us to work within His plan.

In each chapter, I will highlight what God is doing in the lives of Joseph's family and discuss what it teaches us about living our dream. As you read, record what God is saying to you about your dream. I suggest you start a dream journal to record what God has done and is doing in your life. Write down what He says, including words of encouragement and guidance. The goal is not just to understand our dreams but to live them fully engaged with God, our Dream-giver, giving Him the glory He deserves.

At the end of each chapter, I've provided two sections to help you record your insights regarding dreams. In the section I call Dream Notes, I reiterate the main points of each chapter. As you review them, record the ones you need most in your dream journal. Add your own notes as God speaks to you about your dream. In Dream Work, I ask thought-provoking questions to help you discover or continue living your dream. Answer these prayerfully, trusting God as your Dream leader to guide you through your journey.

I'm so excited to walk this path with you and share how God has advanced my God-given dream. I wish I were sitting beside you as you come to the end of each chapter, so I could hear how He has led and encouraged you in your dream. Even though I cannot be with you in person, I know the One who is. Our Dream Giver will be with you all the way. And I trust what God did for Joseph and his family, He will do for you.

Read on, dream walker, your dream awaits. If not before, I'll see you in glory when all dreams are fulfilled.

—Karen Griffin

Chapter 1
Beginning of a Dream

Our God-given dreams started before we were born. It's all part of God's dream. He was working in the world and in you before He created either of us. He created us for His purpose. We were wanted, designed, and made by God to be His children. We're God's dream. As His children, we become part of His dream to bring men and women to Himself. He determines our role in this plan and gives it to us as our God-given dreams.

We see this clearly in the life of Joseph. Rachel longed for and dreamed of having a child. She didn't know it, but God was also dreaming of the child He would send her. He had plans for their family that He would bring about through her dream child. In this, Joseph was God's dream. He planned for Joseph and his life before He created him in Rachel's womb. God was working even when Rachel thought He wasn't.

Rachel's family dynamics were difficult. Jacob loved and chose Rachel to be his wife. After working for seven years to win her hand in marriage, her father tricked him by giving him Leah, her older sister, on their wedding night. Rachel's father then asked Jacob to wait a week and agree to work seven more years to marry Rachel as his second wife (Genesis 29:16-30). Years into the marriage, Leah bore children to Jacob, but Rachel remained childless. She watched as God gave Leah four boys. When Rachel saw she was not bearing children, she became jealous of Leah and demanded Jacob give her children, saying, "Give me children, or I'll die!" Jacob became irritated with Rachel and said God was the one who kept her from having children (Genesis 29:31-30:2).

We often blame others when our dreams seem hindered. We want to think someone else is causing the problem. Our feelings of inadequacy may be too hard to face, so we shift the blame, choose to believe it is their fault, and comfort ourselves by saying, 'If only they would ... then I could ...'

While my dream of being a wife and mother came early for me, my dream to write did not. I first felt the call to write when my kids were toddlers. The busyness of motherhood seemed to prevent me from attaining the dream of becoming an author. I felt barren in this area and had to fight against feelings of 'if only my kids were older.' I also had to resist the temptation to blame others for not helping me, or even God for not providing extra income to hire a sitter to give me extra time to pursue my dream.

In Rachel's case, the truth of who was to blame was God. Many times, when we think others are keeping us from getting what we want, it is God who withholds the desired treasure. Genesis 29:31 says, "When the Lord saw that Leah was not loved, he enabled her to conceive, but Rachel remained childless." God directly says He is the one who enabled Leah to have children. By implication, He shows He allowed Rachel to remain barren.

Rachel did what we tend to do. When her dreams weren't realized, she became jealous of others living their dreams and blamed everyone but herself. It was obvious from the fact Jacob fathered children with Leah that the cause of Rachel's barrenness lay within her own body.

Sometimes, the pain of not receiving what we feel God has promised us causes us to become bitter toward others. As I saw others living the dream of teaching and writing, I was jealous. If I had continued to focus on what others were doing and what I felt I couldn't do, I could have become bitter.

Rachel's pain of not being able to have children also caused her to look at the situation as worse than it was. She says if she does not have children, she will die. Although she felt she would die of a broken heart, she could live without giving birth. Rachel then placed the blame on Jacob because of her inability to deal with the pain.

Do you have an unrealized dream? Are you jealous of others who are already living their dream and blame them for your barrenness? Worse, do you take matters into your own hands?

Rachel did. Seeing she was childless; she hatched a plan to realize her dream the worldly way. If neither Jacob nor God would give her children, she would act to ensure children came to her from Jacob. Rachel took her servant, Bilhah, to her husband and instructed him to sleep with her so she could have children through her. Bilhah became pregnant and gave birth to a son named Dan. Rachel claimed this was her vindication. At the birth of a second son through Bilhah, she claimed she won the war with her sister (Genesis 30:3-6).

Dear ones, we must not do this. Why are we so ready to credit the good things to God and not the bad? Rachel's barrenness and her 'conception' through Bilhah were both directly controlled by God. God allowed the conception of Dan in Bilhah's womb, and He allowed

Rachel to remain barren. God may allow plans we devise to become reality, but the substitute will never satisfy as fully as what God intended.

As I waited for the opportunity to teach God's Word to adults, I poured myself into parenting. I began teaching children's classes because that's what I thought teachers with kids were supposed to do. Although I am grateful for this time with the children and feel like God taught me through them, the experience didn't satisfy my dream to teach God's Word.

In the areas where you feel barren, have you taken matters into your own hands and conceived a backup plan in case God doesn't come through? If so, dear friend, we should ask ourselves, "Do I want a Dan or a Joseph?" The promise is not in Dan. Anything we decide to substitute for what God wants us to have is a substitution. Are we willing to wait for our Joseph, or will we settle for a Dan? The carnal will never live up to the spiritual. What we settled for will never satisfy as much as the promise received.

Do you feel like there is something God is withholding or being slow about providing? Perhaps it's a spouse, a new job, or a ministry opportunity. Are you going to wait for God to work or risk the chance of only having a Dan? It's your choice. If you act without God, He may allow some fruitfulness, but it'll never bring the satisfaction of fulfilling the dream He has for you.

Are you willing to wait for your Joseph? Pray and put it in the hands of the one "who is able to do immeasurably more than all we ask or imagine" (Ephesians 3:20). Rachel claimed she had victory, but did she? Did having children through another woman fulfill her dreams of having her own? Rachel eventually acquired stepchildren, which was a great blessing, but she also shared a husband with two wives and had no child of her own.

In response to the addition to the family, Leah noticed that she stopped bearing children and acted on her own. She took her servant Zilpah and gave her to Jacob, who fathered two boys through her (Genesis 30:9-12). God then blessed Leah again, and she bore two more sons and a daughter (Genesis 30:17-21).

Rachel's earthly plans to fulfill her dreams seemed to backfire, as worldly compromises often do. Jacob now had eleven children: ten boys and one girl, all born to three different women, but Rachel remained childless. Maybe the laughter of small children consoled her longing for her own child, but it is very possible that it inflamed it.

When we see others receiving the favor of the Lord for which we dream, it often drives the longing deeper into our hearts. This, however, may be exactly what God intends to do through the delay of our dreams. As I waited to teach and saw others getting the opportunity, I longed even more to teach for Him.

Barrenness is not uncommon in the Bible. Many men who God would greatly use were born to previously barren women: Isaac to Sarah, Samson to Manoah's wife, Samuel to Hannah, and John the Baptist to Elizabeth. Perhaps God may have delayed giving these children so His role as giver would be fully acknowledged.

We often go through a season of dryness before we receive the dream. When it feels like our dream will never come true, we can turn to God and trust that He is working during our wait. Looking back now on those early years, I see how God had been working in my life, preparing me for the dream He had for me.

Finally, Rachel does what she should have done all along. She cries out to God and trusts the outcome to Him. Genesis 30:22-23 records God's response: "Then God remembered Rachel; he listened to her and enabled her to conceive. She became pregnant and gave birth to a son and said, 'God has taken away my disgrace.'"

At last, the dream is born!

Notice God's actions toward Rachel. He remembered, listened, and enabled. These are the actions we can expect God to take toward us when we entrust our dreams to Him.

This did not mean He ever forgot her. God never forgets one of His children. He is there with us, even when it seems He is not. Isaiah 49:15-16 asks, "Can a mother forget the baby at her breast and have no compassion on the child she has born?" Then answers, "Through she may forget, I will not forget you. See I have engraved you on the palms of my hands."

God was the one who shut the womb of Rachel. When we feel God has denied our dream, the first thing to do is to remind ourselves God loves us. He has a reason for delaying the dream He puts in us. James 1:17 tells us, "Every good and perfect gift is from above, coming down from the Father of the heavenly lights, who does not change like shifting shadows." If our dream is from God, He will deliver it exactly when we need to receive it. Perfect gifts come at ideal times.

In Rachel's case, God sent Joseph at the appointed time. When her barrenness served its purpose, God 'remembered' her and sent her dream.

As I wrote this book, I felt as though God had suddenly remembered the dream, He gave me and was finally beginning to fulfill it. The truth is, He never forgot. He was working all along to prepare me. Now the time is right. He has worked out all the details to make His dream for me a reality.

Delays may be designed for our perfection and maturity. How we respond to them may affect how quickly we are ready to receive the gift. May we accept any delays as perfect gifts and let them have their work in our lives so we may be prepared for our dream when He sends it.

God did not simply say Leah is unloved, I will give her children, and Rachel has plenty of love, so I will give her none. Beloved, God treats us as individuals. He does not base our blessings or the lack of them on someone else's life. Our blessings and the withholding of others depend on what we need as individuals to grow closer to Him and to prepare us for the dreams He has for us. Rachel was barren because her barrenness served a purpose God intended to be fulfilled. When God accomplished His purpose, these words appeared in Scripture: "Then God remembered Rachel" (Genesis 30:22). Dear one, God had not forgotten her. He was aware and ultimately in control of every circumstance in her life. Scripture says He remembered her, meaning God was about to act on her behalf.

Rachel exhausted her worldly attempts before she turned to prayer. First, we saw Rachel turn to her husband; she said to Jacob,

"Give me children or I will die." Next, we saw her turn to Bilhah, her maid, as a human solution to her problem. She received Dan and Naphtali through Bilhah, but she did not find the satisfaction she hoped for. Finally, when she saw nowhere else to turn, she turned to God in prayer.

Are we like Rachel? Isn't our natural tendency to try everything we can to work out a situation? Then, when nothing seems to work, we turn to God and say, "This one is too big for me; God, I need you." Perhaps God responds, "I know it is, and I know you do. I am so pleased you finally realize it." Many times, if God had acted sooner, we would have missed the realization that it was He who solved the problem.

My period of waiting for my dream to come true was a season of learning to pray. Not only did I pray for opportunities to teach for Him, but I also learned to pray about my current opportunities. I learned to ask God whether I should commit to areas of service and to pray for the ability to complete the ones I did. I learned to pray for those whom I served. Before my first conference invitation, I knew I needed to dedicate every aspect to prayer.

If we have been praying faithfully, asking God to act, and the answer still waits, we can be confident God hears. He knows our pain and our desires. In His perfect time, He will act, and we recognize it is all His doing. We will find satisfaction when we receive God's blessing for our lives, not the blessing we desire.

The blessing Rachel received was the very one she sought. When she received it, she also received a greater awareness of her dependence on God and a better understanding of His sovereignty.

Perhaps this revelation initiated what would be further magnified in Joseph's life.

God planned all along to send Himself a servant through the womb of Rachel. Her awaited son, Joseph, would be the one to bring his family to Egypt and save them from a famine. The temporary closing of her womb must have served a purpose. Perhaps God wanted to ensure his birth was directly attributed to Him. He may have waited as He prepared Jacob and Rachel for Joseph's proper upbringing. Maybe Joseph needed to be the younger brother to learn certain character traits.

As I waited through my barren years of not teaching or writing, God was growing me spiritually. I was learning to study and understand the Scripture in a way I could then relate it to others. He was also teaching me patience, dependence, and faithfulness. I needed to trust Him, so I wouldn't be in a position before I was ready for it.

If you are waiting for your dream and wondering if it will ever come true, be comforted knowing the waiting is part of His plan. If you are seeking Him and His will for your life, He will not withhold a blessing unless there is a bigger blessing at stake. We want God to act in our time and way. But we must release Him to act and trust His sovereignty if we are to receive the fullness of the blessing He has for us. He will listen to us, act on our behalf, and deliver the dream when it is His will. He will open the womb and birth the dream at the appointed time.

After many years of barrenness and several failed plans to conceive, Rachel finally received her son. "She named him Joseph, and said, 'May the LORD add to me another son'" (Genesis 30:24).

And indeed, He had. God took away her reproach. The dream was finally born.

However, Rachel would die giving birth to her second dream, Benjamin. Rachel named her firstborn "Joseph, and said, 'May the Lord add to me another son'" (Genesis 35:16-20, 30:24), showing her faith, that God would give her another. Little did she know that in bringing her second son into the world, she would exit it.

How painful this must have been for Joseph. We are not sure how old Joseph was when his mother died, but we know he either experienced the pain of losing his mother or the pain of growing up without one. Being the only child of Rachel at the time of his brother's birth, he suffered the most. His half-brothers by Jacob's other wives would have suffered from the death of a stepmother and aunt. Only Joseph and Benjamin experienced the deep pain of being motherless in a family of many mother figures. Joseph, being the oldest, probably did his best to take up the slack and care for Benjamin while he dealt with the lack of a mother on his own.

Each of us will experience earthly heartache and pain that affects the fulfillment of our dreams. Some of these may be shared by others who can truly relate, but other pains and sorrows will be exclusively ours to bear.

First Peter 1:6-7 explains that our trials are both temporary and necessary. "In all this you greatly rejoice, though now for a little while you may have had to suffer grief in all kinds of trials. These have come so that the proven genuineness of your faith—of greater worth than gold, which perishes even though refined by fire—may result in praise, glory and honor when Jesus Christ is revealed."

Trials are difficult because they are designed to be. They are to be the furnace in our lives purifying us and removing self-assurance and pride. They leave behind dependence on God and build faith to enable us to live our dreams. Suffering may catch us off guard and cause us to lose our vision temporarily. If we cling to our understanding of God, our faith will grow stronger, and we will be prepared to live our dreams to God's honor and glory.

Can you see how past trials, suffering, and heartaches of your life have strengthened and prepared you to live the dream God has given you? Joseph's life will echo this time and time again as he learns to fulfill his God-given purpose. We can learn from his trials and the way he overcomes them.

Dream Notes:

- We all have God-given dreams.
- He created us to live our God-given dreams.
- God controls the advancement of our dreams.
- When our dreams advance slowly, we shouldn't shift the blame, become jealous, or take matters into our own hands.
- Nothing we settle for satisfies as much as achieving our God-given dreams.
- God will reveal and fulfill His dream for us.
- When we pray, we can expect Him to remember, listen, and enable us.
- All circumstances in life strengthen and prepare us to live our God-given dreams.

Dream Work:

- Have you discovered your God-given dream?
- If so, take some time to pray about God using your dream to fulfill His mission.
- Write a statement of commitment to following your God-given dream in your journal.
- Who do you know who has a similar dream?
- How can the path they have laid help you walk your dream path?
- If you have not discovered your dream, ask God to reveal His plan for your life.
- Questions to help you discover your dream:
    - What is your favorite way to serve others?
    - What needs do you notice around you that you want to fulfill?
    - Who do you admire for the way they serve God?
    - Consider asking this person to be your encouragement partner.

Chapter 2
Designed For the Dream

Rachel realized her dream of having a child. She passed away, but her dream lived on. Joseph lived with his father, stepmothers, and siblings. As he grew, so did the love his father had for him. We will see that his father especially favored him, just as we are each favored by our Heavenly Father.

We are each dearly loved by God. He chose us before the world began. He brought us to Himself, forgave us of our sins, and redeemed us by His grace. He continues to perfect us so that we may be holy and blameless in His love. Desiring to become our Father, He adopted each of us as His child. We are completely and irrevocably accepted by Him in our Beloved Jesus. Through Him, He blesses us with every spiritual blessing (Ephesians 1:3-7). In Jeremiah 31:3, God declares, "I have loved you with an everlasting love; I have drawn you with unfailing kindness." Yes, God draws us to Himself, puts His dreams in our hearts, and writes our stories.

Genesis 37 introduces the story of Joseph by saying, "Jacob lived in the land where his father had stayed, the land of Canaan. This is the account of Jacob's family line. Joseph, a young man of seventeen, was" (Genesis 37:1-2). Instead of finding a list of Jacob's descendants to define his family line, we see only one—Joseph. How strange for the text to list him here in this way. Perhaps this was to show the importance of Joseph in his father's line.

As we know, Joseph was born to Rachel after a period of barrenness. But the details of his birth were exactly as God intended. God's perfect plan included his being born to Rachel as the eleventh of twelve sons of Jacob.

The same is true for us. God determined when, where, and to whom each of us was born. Nothing about us or the circumstances of our birth was an accident. God also created each of us physically just as He desired us to be. Psalm 139:13-14 declares, "For you created my inmost being; you knit me together in my mother's womb. I praise you because I am fearfully and wonderfully made; your works are wonderful, I know that full well."

We are exactly the way He designed us to be. He chose our hair color, our eye color, and our skin color. He determined whether we would be short or tall, thin or curvy. Even if we dislike the way we look, we can accept it. We are the way we are by God's design.

He also shaped our basic personality. He decided whether we would be talkative or quiet, planners or spontaneous, introverted or extroverted, leaders or followers. Although our environment can influence these qualities, we all have natural tendencies toward certain personality types.

I have three adult children, each with a unique personality. My oldest daughter started talking when she was nine months old, made her first three-word sentence by one, and hasn't stopped talking since. My son learned very early that he could get what he wanted by pointing and making a grunting sound. He preferred his older sister to talk for him, a task she gladly fulfilled. Even as he got older, he talked only when necessary. I even needed to teach him that it was rude not to respond to others when they said hello. My youngest daughter is a natural-born leader, which is hard to do when you're the youngest. As an adult, she has flourished with her leadership ability.

Thank God for the way He designed you and consider how these traits align with the dream He has given you. But never use them as an excuse to delay pursuing your dream. God created me as a fearful introvert. I have a picture of myself around the age of five, where I look mad. I asked my mom if the picture was taken when I was upset. She said it was the best picture they could get because I was so shy around the photographer.

When God called me to a teaching ministry, I needed to gain confidence to speak publicly, as well as overcome my natural tendency to avoid one-on-one conversations. If I used my shyness as an excuse, I would hinder God from advancing His plans for me. Psalm 139:16 says, "Your eyes saw my unformed body; all the days ordained for me were written in your book before one of them came to be." God has our days planned for us. He created us according to those plans.

Next, we see that Jacob (also named Israel) favored Joseph. "Now Israel loved Joseph more than any of his other sons, because he had been born to him in his old age" (Genesis 37:3). The circumstances of Joseph's birth made him special to his father. He was born to Jacob's favorite wife, who died giving birth to his brother. Reminding Jacob of Rachel, Joseph may have comforted him in his time of sorrow. Jacob's personality may have softened with age causing him to treat Joseph more like a grandchild than a son. Perhaps, he had more time to spend with Joseph than the older brothers.

We also see that at seventeen, Joseph brought a bad report of his brothers' work to his father (Genesis 37:2). At first glance, Joseph may appear to be a tattletale, but Scripture does not indicate whether the report was accurate or not. Judging by the character Joseph later shows and the fact that Jacob later sent Joseph to check on the brothers, we might assume he gave an accurate and necessary report. Joseph was looking out for his father's interests. These factors combine, and we see that Joseph was the favored son.

Just as Jacob especially loved Joseph, our heavenly Father loves us. John 3:16 is a favorite verse for many. "For God so loved the world that he gave his one and only Son, that whoever believes in him shall not perish but have eternal life." We love this verse and encourage others to memorize it because it assures us of God's love. One of the greatest desires of any person is to be loved, and we have a heavenly Father who loves us.

God loves us more than anyone on this earth can. John 15:13 says, "Greater love has no one than this: to lay down one's life for one's friends." Jesus willingly laid down His life for us. Romans 5:8 says, "But God demonstrates his own love for us in this: While we were still sinners, Christ died for us." God loved us so much that He let His beloved Son die for us, even when we were still His enemies.

Early in my Christian walk, I wondered if God loved me as much as He loved others. Although I believed in His sacrificial love, I still questioned whether He liked me. I saw His love more like pity than genuine love. I also thought love was based on goodness. When I observed others living more righteously and serving more faithfully, I assumed God must have loved them more than He loved me. I failed to recognize the vastness of the love He had for me.

We may not feel loved. Having been mistreated by loved ones, neglected by companions, or abused by those we trusted may have skewed our view of love. I pray as the apostle Paul prayed, that you "may have power … to grasp how wide and long and high and deep is the love of Christ, and to know this love that surpasses knowledge" (Ephesians 3:18-19). First John 4:8 says God is love. God is, in His being, the essence of love. He can't cease loving us. He loves us with an everlasting love (Jeremiah 31:3). Before He formed us in the womb, He knew us (Jeremiah 1:5). He knows the number of hairs on our heads (Matthew 10:30). He chooses us and calls us by our names (Isaiah 45:4). Because of the love He gives us, we are now the children of God (1 John 3:1).

My friend, God loves you. He loves you more than anyone else loves you. He loves you fully and completely. Look at how Jesus describes His love for us in John 15:9. He says, "As the Father has loved me, so have I loved you." Do you doubt how much God the Father loved Jesus, His Son? Then, do not doubt how much Jesus loves you. He loved you enough to die for you so you could become part of His family. His love for you includes a desire for fellowship. He has always and will always love you. There is nothing you have done or will do to stop Him from loving you. Romans 8:38-39 assures us, "For I am convinced that neither death nor life, neither angels nor demons, neither the present nor the future, nor any powers, neither height nor depth, nor anything else in all creation, will be able to separate us from the love of God that is in Christ Jesus our Lord."

I pray that you're fully convinced of God's love for you and feel chosen and special to Him. He created you for a relationship and paid the ultimate price to regain it when sin destroyed it. He has special plans for you. It's imperative to believe this to walk in your God-given dream. If you struggle with fully believing God loves you, spend some time in prayer asking God to manifest His love to you so clearly that you will embrace it.

Jacob showed his special love for Joseph by giving him "an ornate robe" (Genesis 37:3). This special gift confirmed to the brothers that Joseph was the favorite son and caused them to hate him. "Now Israel loved Joseph more than any of his other sons, because he had been born to him in his old age; and he made an ornate robe for him. When his brothers saw their father loved him more than any of them, they hated him and could not speak a kind word to him" (Genesis 37:3-4).

This is a poor model for parenthood, but an excellent example of God's love for us. He loves each of us so much. He shows it by clothing us in righteousness. "God made him who had no sin to be sin for us, so that in him we might become the righteousness of God" (2 Corinthians 5:21). He makes us beautiful by clothing us with Himself. At salvation, the Holy Spirit of God enters us to transform and equip us.

In a parable told by Jesus in Luke 15, a son took his inheritance while the father was still living and squandered it on unrighteous living. After running out of money and becoming so desperate that he had to feed swine, he decided to go home and beg his father to make him a servant. When he returned home wearing garments soiled and smelly from the pigpen, the father immediately commanded, "Bring the best robe and put it on him. Put a ring on his finger and sandals on his feet" (Luke 15:22).

Like Jacob and the father of the prodigal son, our heavenly Father shows His love for us by clothing us in His finest. We are "conformed into the image of his Son" (Romans 8:29) through the power of the Spirit. Through this, He created us spiritually just as He wants us to be.

Over the years, I have learned to recognize some of the character traits God has given me. He made me accepting of others and gave me a desire to listen to and help others. Through His help, I learned communication skills and conquered my fear of public speaking. Thanks to Him, I focus less on myself and have learned to prioritize serving others. He has molded me to fulfill His plans for me.

Second Corinthians 5:17 says, "Therefore, if anyone is in Christ, the new creation has come: The old has gone, the new is here!" Our old habits, ways of thinking, and attitudes are discarded. Anything not lining up with the dreams God has given us is removed. God re-creates those parts of us sin has tainted to beautify and cleanse us. He clothes us with favor to signify the love He has for us. Unlike Joseph, who stood out from his brothers, we stand collectively dressed in favor among our sisters and brothers. God loves each of us uniquely and individually. With Him, we are all favored, and He dresses us accordingly.

Ephesians 2:10 indicates God recreates us at salvation to match the dreams He has given us. "For we are God's handiwork, created in Christ Jesus to do good works, which God prepared in advance for us to do." By using the words "in Christ," this verse points to the second creation we experience at our salvation. At salvation, God recreates us, giving us new desires and ways of thinking. He gifts us with the spiritual gifts we need to fulfill His dreams.

We think God looks at us, evaluates our abilities, and then decides what He wants us to do. According to Ephesians 2:10, He prepared our works "in advance." God decides what He wants to do, then He creates a person to accomplish His purpose. The work God has planned becomes the dreams He puts in us to do His will.

Sometimes we look at ourselves, evaluate our abilities, and forget that God created us perfectly for the tasks He has assigned to us. We may look at ourselves and say, "There's nothing special about me. I'm average in attractiveness, intelligence, and abilities. Everything about me is mediocre." To ourselves and the world, we may appear average, but to God, we're unique in every way. He gave us the personality He wanted us to have, designed us perfectly to fit His purpose, and gave us the gifts and talents to realize our dreams.

If you struggled to feel loved and chosen by God, review the story of God appointing David as king of Israel in First Samuel 16. God sent Samuel to Bethlehem to anoint one of Jesse's sons to be the next king. Jesse brought his oldest son, Eliab, to Samuel. He was convinced from his appearance that he must be the one God chose. "But the LORD said to Samuel, 'Do not consider his appearance or his height, for I have rejected him. The LORD does not look at the things people look at. People look at the outward appearance, but the LORD looks at the heart'" (1 Samuel 16:7). God does not see as man sees. We can stop listening to the world because what God says about us matters most.

One by one, Jesse brought his seven oldest sons to Samuel. One by one, God indicated none of them was the one. Finally, in desperation, Jesse brought his youngest from the field and presented him to Samuel. David stood before him bright-eyed, tanned from the sun, dressed in his shepherd's clothes, looking like a kid and smelling like a sheep. God announced, "Rise and anoint him; this is the one" (1 Samuel 16:12).

God didn't care that David was a shepherd or the youngest. God knew exactly who he was. He created him and put him exactly where He wanted him. God used all this (being the youngest and being a shepherd) to prepare him to be the future king of Israel. And I believe the moment Samuel anointed him, the dream of becoming king was birthed in David's heart. God would spend the next decade and a half cultivating the dream and preparing David to fulfill it.

When we discover our dreams and ask how or why and question our abilities, we can choose to acknowledge that God has uniquely designed us for it. We can respond as Mary did, "I am the Lord's servant … May your word to me be fulfilled" (Luke 1:38). The purpose of this book is to help us recognize and realize our God-given dreams.

Maybe we don't feel chosen for big dreams. Those around us might think God would never choose us. But what God sees and says matters.

Dream Notes:

- God loves each of us dearly.
- God determined when, where, and to whom we would be born.
- God designed us physically just the way He wanted us to be.
- God gave us the personality He wanted us to have and continues to shape it to match our dreams.
- God chose us to fulfill the dreams He gave us.
- God clothes all believers in righteousness through Jesus.
- His Spirit transforms us and equips us to live our dreams.

Dream Work:

- How has God created you uniquely from those around you?
- Make a list of the qualities God has given you.
- Which of these will help you fulfill your dream?
- Prayerfully, make a list of areas where God is challenging you to grow.
- Ask God to cultivate the Christ-like qualities you need to fulfill your dream.
- Do you feel loved and accepted by God?
- If you struggle with this, study Ephesians 1, focusing on who God says you are.
- How can you help others experience this same love?

Chapter 3
Discovering the Dream

We have seen how Joseph was the fulfillment of his mother Rachel's dream and how his father favored and cherished him. Now we will see God give Joseph a dream revealing future events affecting Joseph and his family.

Just as God acted in Joseph's life, He operates in ours. He endows us with desires, ideas, and creativity. He sparks dreams in us, paralleling His plans for us. Whether we have discovered our dreams, God knows them. He authored them, and He acts in our lives to reveal and fulfill them. As we live our lives for Him, we will discover the dreams God has for us.

Quickly in Joseph's story, Scripture reveals his God-given dream. Although it would be many years before he understood its whole meaning, he recognized it was from God. Genesis 37:5 begins, "Joseph had a dream."

While this may seem unique, we all have dreams. God places in us a desire to accomplish and be productive in life. He provides us with ideas and plans. As children, we often dream of what we want to become when we grow up, and then work to achieve those dreams as we mature. Even if we aren't sure what we want to do, most of us desire to be productive and feel our lives matter.

My dream is to teach others to be rooted in the truth of God's Word and live with purpose, fulfilling their God-given dreams. I seek to live my dream by teaching in churches, speaking at conferences, and writing books and Bible studies.

Living the dream may not be easy, as we will see with Joseph, but it burns inside of us, pushing us toward God's plan for our lives. Have you discovered your God-given dream? Are you actively pursuing it? Watching Joseph discover and realize his dream will inspire us to pursue our own.

Joseph dreamed about his future and informed his brothers. "Joseph had a dream, and when he told it to his brothers, they hated him all the more ... Listen to this dream I had: We were binding sheaves of grain out in the field when suddenly my sheaf rose and stood upright, while your sheaves gathered around mine and bowed down to it" (Genesis 37:5-7). Joseph and his brothers recognized that the dream meant one day Joseph would rule over them.

Joseph didn't create his dream — God gave it to him. He was probably just as surprised as his brothers when he first woke up and thought about what it meant. Being the youngest in the family usually meant a role of service, not glory, but this dream was from God. It was a sign of what was to come. We might not receive dreams while we sleep, but most of us envision our future. God created us for a purpose and gives us desires to fulfill His plans.

Other biblical characters dreamed about accomplishing acts of service for God. When Nehemiah heard that the walls of Jerusalem were in ruins, he was deeply saddened. He dreamed of traveling to Jerusalem and helping rebuild the walls. He received permission and funds from King Artaxerxes I to proceed with repairing the walls.

Despite opposition from the enemy, he led the effort to rebuild them in fifty-two days (Nehemiah 1:1-4, 2:4-8, 6:15).

Hannah, like Joseph's mother Rachel, dreamed of having a child but remained childless while her husband's other wife had children. Distraught with desire, she poured out her plea to God for a son and promised to give him into God's service. God showed favor to her and granted her dream by sending Samuel, who would become a prophet in Israel (1 Samuel 1).

The Holy Spirit revealed to a devout man named Simeon that he would see the long-awaited Messiah before he died. This must have become Simeon's dream. Each day, he might have entered the temple wondering if it would be the day the Promised One would arrive. At last, on the appointed day, led by the Spirit, he entered the temple and encountered Mary, Joseph, and baby Jesus. "Simeon took him in his arms and praised God, saying: 'Sovereign Lord, as you have promised, you may now dismiss your servant in peace. For my eyes have seen your salvation'" (Luke 2:28-30).

Our dreams may be less dramatic than those of these Biblical characters. We might have dreamed of becoming a doctor, nurse, firefighter, or teacher. For as long as we can remember, this has been the only profession we've ever desired. Or perhaps we've always felt compassion for the elderly, children, or people in poverty. Others of us may have been drawn to a foreign country or wished to be missionaries. My dream began with a passion for studying God's Word, which turned into a desire to teach it. As I taught in my local church, I dreamed of teaching others at conferences and retreats.

Writing my lesson plans for Sunday school grew my desire to write full-length Bible studies and Christian living books.

Some of us may not recognize our dreams until we live them. Circumstances push us into a particular area or job. As we work to support ourselves and our families, we realize we are living the dream God has put within us. For others, their dreams may not involve their jobs, other than providing the funds for them. We may live or pursue our dreams in the evenings or on weekends. Our dreams may be lived out serving others at our church on Sundays. It may also comprise minor acts of service.

If we have not yet discovered the dreams God has for us, we can ask Him. As we listen carefully for His leading, He'll reveal what He wants us to do. Step-by-step obedience to Him guides us toward our God-given dreams, even if we are unaware of it.

One way to recognize our dreams is to reflect on what we strive to accomplish in our lives. How do we want to serve God? If we didn't have to work at a job and money were no object, what would we do for God? Answering these questions provides us with a clear understanding of our dreams. Then we can ask God, "How can I pursue this dream with the limited time and resources I have?" He will guide us and provide what we need for the dream He has for us. If we think we know the dream, we can ask Him if we are hearing correctly and heading in the right direction.

In the early stages of living my dream, I repeatedly asked God to confirm that His plan for me was to write. He reassured me by increasing my desire to teach, by having others share how my teaching helped them, and by leading others to invite me to speak at their church. At the first writer's conference I attended, I only knew that I wanted to write. Upon arrival, I was instructed to schedule meetings with field experts. Hoping to open a door—any door —I made appointments without knowing who anyone was. I met a kind older man who read a sample of my writing and told me I was a talented writer. Later that week, I was amazed to find out that the man who had praised me was being honored for his accomplishments in the publishing industry. I hadn't realized I had chosen such a notable person in the industry to review my writing. God used this man's praise to confirm that He has indeed called and equipped me to write for Him.

Dreams often consume our thoughts. I imagine Joseph wondered if the dream truly came from God. He might have thought about it often and prayed about it. God confirmed His message to Joseph through a second dream. This time, the sun, moon, and eleven stars were bowing down to him (Genesis 37:9).

Joseph's second dream was like the first. This time, instead of his brothers' sheaves of wheat, celestial objects bowed to him. Through this dream, God confirmed what He planned for Joseph's life. Joseph may have wondered about the details, but he probably understood he would rise above his family. Dreaming it twice reinforced it was from God.

These perplexing dreams spurred thoughts and questions in his mind. As he pondered their meaning, he felt compelled to share his thoughts. Perhaps after his brother's reaction to his original dream, Joseph hesitated to reveal the second one. He must have known they would not be happy to hear their little brother was dreaming about ruling over them. He may have tried to keep the dream to himself, but he couldn't.

He might have naively thought they would be pleased to hear one of them would be a ruler, even if it were their younger brother. Maybe he hoped they would recognize it was God's plan and submit to it. Pride may have also played a part in Joseph's sharing. Sensing his brothers' dislike of him, Joseph might have shared his dreams with them to prove even God thought he was special.

As our dreams grow, we may want to share them with others but hesitate because we fear their reactions. We can confidently share, as we guard against pride and ensure we have the right motives. Revealing our God-given dreams to others allows them to pray for us and encourage us. When I dreamed of being a writer, I feared sharing my desire with others. I thought they might think I had an over-inflated ego, thinking I could write a book. I also feared the embarrassment I would experience if I failed. However, to move forward, it was wise to disclose my dream to my family, so they could support me and understand why I spent so much time studying. It was also helpful to meet others with the same dream so they could encourage me along the way.

Even when I signed the publishing agreement for this book, I feared announcing it. I was afraid something would happen, and my dream would continue to go unrealized. I needed to take courage, speak in faith, and take the first step to make it happen.

As God reveals our dreams, they grow and become difficult to suppress. The desire He puts in us propels us toward the mission God has for us. It often swells inside of us until we must reveal it. Our God-given dreams will persist until we reveal and act on them.

God declared to His people, "For I know the plans I have for you … plans to prosper you and not to harm you, plans to give you hope and a future" (Jeremiah 29:11). If we are children of God, He has plans for us. He has determined the part each of us is to play in advancing His kingdom. As we obediently follow Him, He'll reveal the steps we are to take to fulfill those plans.

First, God calls us into a relationship with Him, as we saw reflected in the special love Jacob had for Joseph. Second, He calls us to His service. As Jacob gave shepherding to his sons, God has called us to help others.

Our tasks may be different, but we serve with one common goal—to glorify God, our Father. We glorify Him as we obey His word, testify and minister to those around us, and worship Him in truth. Completing the tasks He gives us on the path to our dreams also glorifies Him.

Some tasks God calls us to do are universal–loving others, witnessing, and ministering to those in need. Others are specific to us as individuals–caring for a chronically ill family member, being a Christian influence at our workplace, or serving in a particular ministry. Some are long-term, such as being a godly mother, friend, and wife, or being called to teach or serve in the mission field. Others are short-term, such as calling to encourage a friend, cooking a meal for someone, or volunteering for a special event. Each task God assigns is a steppingstone in the building of our dreams.

Big dreams frequently result from many smaller ones. Each of our assigned tasks builds to the fulfillment of the specific dream God has given us. Every assignment is important and is an opportunity to serve and honor Him. Obeying Him in all areas leads us along the dream path and helps us arrive at the destination where we are living the dream.

I've taken many steps toward my dream of becoming a Christian author. By accepting the classes offered to me, I learned to teach. I practiced writing and meeting deadlines by blogging regularly. Listening and sharing with other ladies taught me people skills.

God sometimes surprises us with the tasks He assigns, and we may feel inadequate to perform them. However, we should decide in advance if God calls us to a job, we will do it because it's His will.

Think about Mary, the mother of Jesus. She was a young girl with hopes and dreams for her future. Her plans probably did not include becoming pregnant and being accused of being an immoral woman. Yet, when the angel informed her that she would be the mother of Christ, she responded in obedience: "I am the Lord's servant … May your word to me be fulfilled" (Luke 1:38).

When we sense God is calling us to a task, we can resist questioning our ability and respond like Mary. Instead of asking how or why, we can say, "Yes, Lord, I am your servant. Let Your plans for me come true. Use me however You want to use me." We trust Him to fulfill the dream. "In their hearts humans plan their course, but the LORD establishes their steps" (Proverbs 16:9). When we learn to take the steps God instructs, we will advance toward the dream He has for us. We can trust He will work all things out as we obediently follow

Him. After all, it's God's dream we want to fulfill, not our own. He is the one who knows what needs to be done to accomplish it. God assures us, "I will instruct you and teach you in the way you should go; I will counsel you with my loving eye on you" (Psalm 32:8).

God may not speak to us directly through a dream as He did to Joseph, but He will lead us in the direction He wants us to go. Through the Holy Spirit, He puts His dreams in us. Then He guides us as we walk along our dream paths. Jesus promised the Spirit would guide us, teach us, and remind us of the things we need to know (John 14:26, 16:13).

God has faithfully guided me through the years. With each step of obedience I took, I learned to follow my Dream Leader carefully as He directed me down the path He had chosen.

Sometimes we may doubt whether we know our God-given dreams. We may ask ourselves, "What if I've heard God wrong? What if He didn't give me this dream?"

We can trust God will guide us. God told Samuel He was looking for "a man after his own heart" to replace Saul as king (1 Samuel 13:14). He is looking for the same type of people today–not ones who know everything and always make the right choices, but those who trust Him and want to do His will. Do we trust Him enough to believe He will redirect us if we head in the wrong direction?

Isaiah 30:21 says, "Whether you turn to the right or to the left, your ears will hear a voice behind you, saying, 'This is the way; walk in it.'" We can choose to walk confidently, trusting God will lead us and redirect us if we head down the wrong path. He will lead us to our dreams.

The Apostle Paul is a great example of this. He dreamed of taking the gospel to Spain (Romans 15:24), but there is no biblical evidence he ever made it. Perhaps he desired to go to Spain, but God's actual dream for him was to go to Rome. We certainly would never think of Paul as having failed his dream. It is very probable that God redirected his steps and sent him exactly where He wanted him.

I pray you've recognized your God-given dreams and are taking the steps He is directing to fulfill them. Take courage, fellow dream-walker, we are in this together. As we walk along with Joseph, we will see his and our dreams become realities.

Dream Notes:

- God gives us all dreams and directs us toward them.
- God created us for a purpose and gives us desires to achieve His plans.
- God sparks dreams in us, paralleling His plans for us and propelling us toward our mission.
- As we live our lives for Him, we will discover the dreams God has for us.
- When God reveals our dreams, we should carefully listen for His directions and obey as He leads us toward our dreams.
- God brings us into a relationship with Him and then calls us to serve Him through our dreams.
- Big dreams frequently result from many smaller dreams.
- Circumstances may push us toward our God-given dreams.
- God will redirect us if we head down the wrong path.

Dream Work:

- If you know your God-given dream, consider writing a purpose statement in your dream journal.

- How far have you come along your dream path?

- Make a list of your dream accomplishments to serve as encouragement when your dream path gets rocky.

- How can you bravely share your dream with others?

- Choose at least two people with whom to share your dream and ask them to pray for you.

- If you're still seeking to discover your dream, commit to praying daily for God to reveal it.

- Consider the ways God has already used you. Do you see a pattern emerging?

- Consider taking a spiritual gifts test.

Chapter 4
Death of a Dream

Our dream paths may not be easy. Even when we are obediently following God's plan, obstacles can lie in the path of our dreams. There may be times when we question whether we have heard our dreams correctly or when it appears our dreams are dead. Rest assured, fellow dreamer, no one except us can stop a dream God has designated for us.

Joseph would face many hindrances on the long path to actualizing his dream, the first of which would be his brothers. When Joseph told them his first dream, they asked, "Do you intend to reign over us?" They hated him even more because of it. When he dreamed a second time, he told his brothers and his father. His father rebuked him, and his brothers became jealous (Genesis 37:8-11).

Although anger and jealousy consumed his brothers, they must have sensed God revealing the future. They were jealous Joseph received the dream and hated him for its meaning. Later, we see their rage and envy caused them to take action to prevent the dream from coming true.

Others may question our dreams or our motives. When Joseph's father heard Joseph's dream, he asked, "What is this dream you had?" Jacob could not fathom Joseph would rule over the entire family (Genesis 37:10).

When we become brave enough to share our dreams, we should be prepared. Not everyone will understand or believe in our dreams. Although God may send supporters who encourage us to pursue our dreams, others may be uninterested. They may not understand why we are so passionate about our missions and may even discourage us. When others doubt or question our dreams, we can use them as a reason to pray for confirmation from God. We can trust Him to lead us because the dreams we are seeking to fulfill are His.

In my dream of becoming an author, some have asked me why I invest so much time in an endeavor that doesn't always yield a monetary profit. They don't understand that living the dream isn't about what we get out of it, but about fulfilling the dreams God has put in us.

Joseph's brothers understood that the dream of their sheaves bowing down to Joseph's meant he would one day rule over them. In a society where birth order ruled, they must have thought their little brother was delusional. They resisted believing it could be true and questioned its validity.

Jacob's response to the second dream confirmed its meaning, but he rebuked Joseph for telling it. Even Jacob, himself a dreamer, had a hard time believing Joseph's dream was from God. How could Joseph rule over his whole family? But Jacob kept the matter in mind (Genesis 37:10-11).

We can fight discouragement when others don't believe in our dreams. After all, they're our dreams, not theirs. They have their own dreams, even if they haven't discovered them yet.

Those who have dreams and are living them are often the ones who will encourage us to follow ours. Since God had previously spoken to Jacob in dreams (Genesis 28:10-22), he was more likely to believe that Joseph was hearing from God.

When we need encouragement to follow our God-given dreams, we can look to those who are firmly on the path to theirs. They will encourage us. Regardless of our dreams, there's probably someone we know with similar dreams. If not, we can reach out and find them.

As I lived my dream of teaching God's Word, I connected with other teachers and learned from them. As I felt led to write, I went to writers' conferences and met many who also dreamed of writing books to help others see Jesus. Many have encouraged me and helped me along my path.

God, as our Dream-giver, will be our best encourager. We can ask Him to increase our faith, build our confidence, and heighten our desire to pursue our dreams. It's best to stay in constant contact with Him as our Dream Coach so He can direct and re-direct our steps when necessary.

Scripture is a perpetual source of encouragement. For example, Isaiah 58:11 says, "The LORD will guide you always; he will satisfy your needs in a sun-scorched land and will strengthen your frame. You will be like a well-watered garden, like a spring whose waters never fail." Though our dream paths may be long and trying, we can expect God to guide us and provide what we need. Even when it feels like we are in a desert, God will refresh us along the way. We can remind ourselves that a desert may be the path leading toward our dreams.

Joseph was about to find himself marching through a desert on the way to his dream. One day, Jacob sent Joseph to check on his brothers, who were shepherding their flock. Joseph obediently headed out to Shechem as his father instructed. When he could not find them, he asked and found they had moved on to Dothan. He faithfully continued his journey to complete his mission (Genesis 37:12-17).

The brothers spotted Joseph's coat of many colors coming from a mile away, and they devised a plan to stop Joseph and his dream. They maliciously planned to kill their brother, throw his body in a pit, and claim a ferocious animal killed him. All to stop his dream. They said to each other, "Then we'll see what comes of his dreams" (Genesis 37:18-20).

Hatred and jealousy are powerful motivators. Our enemy, Satan, wants nothing more than to kill us, damn us, and send us to the same fiery fate awaiting him. Since God has prevented him from doing so by sealing us with His Holy Spirit, Satan conspires to do all he can to hinder us in our earthly life.

John 10:10 says, "The thief comes only to steal and kill and destroy." Satan wants to destroy our dreams. He attempts to steal opportunities to advance in the dreams through distraction and kill our desire to move forward with discouragement. He would destroy the dream altogether if he could, just as Joseph's brothers attempted to do to his dreams.

Satan may send saboteurs to frustrate God's plans for us intentionally. Satan would use Judas, one of Jesus's disciples, to betray him to the religious leaders who planned to kill Him (Matthew 26:14-16). Others may act unintentionally. When Jesus talked about his suffering and coming death on the cross, Peter warned Him not to say such things. Jesus rebuked Peter by saying, "Get behind me, Satan! You are a stumbling block to me; you do not have in mind the concerns of God, but merely human concerns" (Matthew 16:23). Even Peter, a true disciple, at that moment was being used by Satan as a saboteur.

Others may try to sabotage our dreams by questioning whether God is the author of them. They may refuse to help us and even discourage us. Whether or not they do it intentionally, we can recognize Satan is the one behind the plan and resist listening to anyone who tries to discourage us from our dreams. God is the One we are to listen to for instructions about fulfilling our God-given dreams.

I faced several attempts at discouragement from others as God led me to teach for Him. I was told at a previous church that we didn't need ladies' classes, that I shouldn't encourage others to follow their dreams, and that only ladies over fifty years old should be teachers. A church once offered me a position leading the women's ministry. I asked to have a couple of weeks to pray about it. Two weeks later, when I called to accept, they informed me the position was filled.

These things could have discouraged me, and I might have given up on my dream, but I viewed them as detours, not roadblocks. And I believe God used each of them to redirect my path and grow me toward my dream. For example, when I was informed that ladies' classes weren't needed at my church, I opened my home on Thursday nights to women who wanted to study together. God used it to reach women in and outside of my church. The home setting helped attendees feel more comfortable and connect on a deeper level.

God controls our dreams and their fulfillment. Satan can do only what God allows him to do. For Joseph, God used Reuben to spare his life. He persuaded the other brothers to adopt a less violent plan. Planning to rescue Joseph later, he suggested they throw Joseph in a pit (Genesis 37:21-22). They would leave Joseph to starve or die from the elements, thus preventing them from having actual blood on their hands.

"So when Joseph came to his brothers, they stripped him of his robe … and they took him and threw him into the cistern. The cistern was empty; there was no water in it." The brothers then sat down to eat, and a caravan of traders passed by on their way to Egypt. Judah convinced the other brothers to sell Joseph to the traders for money, instead of killing him (Genesis 37:23-27).

After selling Joseph for twenty shekels of silver, the brothers took Joseph's robe, dipped it in the blood of goats, took it to their father, and presented it as evidence a wild beast had killed Joseph. Jacob mourned Joseph for many days and refused to be comforted by his other children. He even vowed to mourn until he died. All the while, his brothers kept the secret Joseph was alive (Genesis 37:28-35).

Meanwhile, Joseph was being taken to be sold as a slave in Egypt. Think about how he must have felt after being betrayed by those closest to him. He probably experienced a shock from the betrayal at first. He begged and pleaded with them to let him out when he was in the pit (Genesis 42:21). With each step away from his homeland, discouragement likely grew until he finally felt hopeless. He was headed for a life of slavery or worse, unsure of what his future held. Joseph must have been plagued with doubts about his dreams ever becoming reality. He probably wondered if he would see his family again and whether he'd been mistaken or delusional when he dreamed of them bowing before him.

Joseph didn't realize it, but God was guiding him on the path to fulfill his dream. Similar events might happen to us on our journey toward our goals. Although we might not be thrown into a pit and sold into slavery, we may face situations that shout, "Your dream is dead!" However, Satan can't kill your dreams. Only God can, and why would He give us a dream just to destroy it? Still, God might allow us to go through circumstances that seem to move in the opposite direction of our dreams. When this happens, we can remind ourselves that we might be headed in the 'right' wrong direction. Even though Joseph seemed to move farther from his dream, God was using his brothers' evil intentions to move Joseph to the place where his dream would come true.

God often uses adversity to move us forward and prepare us for our future. James 1:2-4 bids us to "Consider it pure joy … whenever you face trials of many kinds, because you know that the testing of your faith produces perseverance. Let perseverance finish its work so that you may be mature and complete, not lacking anything." God allows some challenges to grow our faith and teach us perseverance. These trials mature us and get us ready to live our dreams.

Financial trials have taught me to trust God to provide for me, as I've never gone without a home or food. Relationship challenges have taught me the importance of compromise and forgiveness. Accusations of not caring about a friend have shown me that motives can be misunderstood, and I need to choose my words carefully. Although I didn't see these situations as joyful at the time, I have learned to be thankful for all circumstances because God uses them to teach me. First Peter 5:10 promises "God ... after you have suffered a little while, will himself restore you and make you strong, firm and steadfast." And Romans 5:3-5 teaches us that suffering "produces perseverance; perseverance, character; and character, hope." These traits will help us walk along our dream paths. Strength will help us keep going when the going gets tough. Firmness and steadfastness will give us confidence to move in whatever direction God chooses. Persevering through difficult situations grows our character and prepares us to live our dreams with integrity. Placing our hope in God and trusting Him to fulfill our dreams, we will walk the paths He has designed for us.

Early in my ministry, I taught Sunday morning classes but started to experience extreme fatigue. This led me to miss many evening services at our church. I didn't feel safe driving when I was so exhausted. After a while, I was asked to step down if I couldn't attend all the services. I didn't know what was wrong with me medically; I just knew I was constantly tired. It felt like I was being punished for something beyond my control. After visiting several doctors, I discovered I had suffered a cortisol crash, was deficient in vitamin D, and had sleep apnea. It was a wonder I was functioning at all.

Another time, I faced fatigue—I'd just agreed to teach at a conference. My topic was about the unstoppable power of the Holy Spirit living within us. Each day, as I lay on the couch feeling unable to move, I would pray and ask God to activate His power in me and help me prepare for my lesson. He did, and I learned firsthand what I was planning to teach at the conference–even if we can't, God can. He empowers and energizes us to do whatever He calls us to do. Through this, I learned that I could always hope in Him, even when I felt incapable.

The obstacles we face along the way may strengthen us and prepare us to achieve our dreams. We see this was the case with Joseph. He learned a great deal during his time of service while waiting for the dream to be realized, as we will. We can choose to keep marching forward, even when it seems we are leaving our dreams behind.

Dream Notes:

- No one except us can stop the dreams God has designated for us.
- Although our dream paths may not be easy, we can trust our Dream-giver to lead us toward our dreams.
- Our Dream-giver, Scripture, and those living their dreams can serve as sources of encouragement as we live ours.
- Satan conspires to do all he can to hinder and destroy our dreams.
- Satan may use others to attempt to sabotage God's plans.
- God uses obstacles and adversity that seem to block our paths to strengthen us and prepare us to live our dreams.
- God alone controls our dreams and their fulfillment. Satan can do only what God allows him to do.

- Following God ensures we are always headed in the right direction.

Dream Work:

- Record moments when it felt like your dream was dead in your dream journal.
- How did you overcome these difficult times?
- If you currently feel you are in the desert between discovering your dream and living it, write a statement in your journal reminding yourself that God is in control of every step you take.
- Begin a list of encouraging scriptures to meditate on when you feel discouraged.
- Here are a few to get you started:
  - "Commit to the LORD whatever you do, and he will establish your plans" (Proverbs 16:3).
  - "This is what the Lord says—your Redeemer, the Holy One of Israel: "I am the Lord your God, who teaches you what is best for you, who directs you in the way you should go'" (Isaiah 48:17).
  - "The LORD makes firm the steps of the one who delights in him" (Psalm 37:23).

Chapter 5
Dream Delays

We last saw Joseph marching toward Egypt, unknowingly moving toward his dream. How would he deal with the death of his dream? Would he give up on the God who he thought spoke to him?

The path to our dreams doesn't always appear as a straight, smooth path. It twists and turns, ascending and descending. As we will see with Joseph, the attitude with which we continue along the way is often more important than the speed at which we proceed.

Many dreamers experience a delay between recognizing and realizing their dreams. Joseph was seventeen when he first dreamed of ruling over his family, but it would be over twenty years before the dream was fulfilled (Genesis 37:2, 41:46, 53, 45:6).

Other biblical characters also faced delays. David was a young man when he was anointed king of Israel and began his reign years later at thirty (1 Samuel 16, 2 Samuel 5:4). Abraham and Sarah waited twenty-five years for the birth of their promised son, Isaac (Genesis 12:2-4, 21:5). Rachel dreamed of becoming a mother but waited many years before God blessed her with Joseph (Genesis 29:31-30:24). Elizabeth also longed for a child and remained childless for years before she conceived John the Baptist (Luke 1:7-13). When Paul was called to preach, he desired to meet with the other apostles, but he waited three years before going up to Jerusalem (Galatians 1:15-18).

I've experienced delays on my path to my dream of speaking and writing. When I first felt led to teach, I was in my early twenties with three small children, so I was much more readily accepted as a children's teacher. Further along in my teaching journey, my husband and I felt led to change churches. People had to get to know me at the new church before I was asked to teach. Even in the writing of this book, I faced delays. I first desired to write about Joseph when my kids were little. I studied and made notes, but the timing never seemed right to write the book. Now, some fifteen years later, I'm finally living this part of my dream.

Joseph's second major obstacle to his dream was a life of servitude. "Now Joseph had been taken down to Egypt. Potiphar, an Egyptian who was one of Pharaoh's officials, the captain of the guard, bought him from the Ishmaelites who had taken him there" (Genesis 39:1). From dreams of exaltation to the reality of slavery, Joseph could have easily become discouraged with his new lot in life.

Joseph may have thought this was the death of his dream. How could someone sold by his brothers into slavery in a foreign land live to see those same brothers bow down to him? But Joseph accepted the delay and move forward with whatever God's new plan for him was.

We can look to Joseph and remind ourselves God-given dreams never die. Knowing God does what He plans to do helps us face delays with faith. We can give our delays to God and trust Him to fulfill the dreams He has for us.

Joseph didn't try to make his dream come true. He couldn't, so he accepted what appeared to be God's new plan. By this point, he probably resigned himself to a life of slavery and doubted his dream was from God. If he ever thought about it, he might have questioned God but tried to trust Him to fulfill it.

It's not uncommon to question God when things go awry. Job questioned God's justice and fairness in the face of immense suffering. He even asked God why He allowed him to be born (Job 3:11). Habakkuk questioned why God tolerated evil (Habakkuk 1:3). Gideon questioned God's calling of him and asked God to prove it (Judges 6:33-40).

We're not the first, nor will we be the last, to struggle to believe God's plan for our life when circumstances scream otherwise. Facing our delays with faith can be challenging, but we can encourage ourselves by reading the Bible. We can learn from those who have also faced delays but continued until they saw the fulfillment of their dreams.

One of the most profound examples of someone having faith amid the death of his dream is Abraham. When instructed by God to take his only son, Isaac, to Mt. Moriah and sacrifice him, Abraham obeyed (Genesis 22). He raised the knife to his son, but trusted God would keep His promise even if it required, He raise Isaac from the dead (Hebrews 11:19).

We can trust our dreams to God. If they are truly God-given dreams, He will fulfill them in His perfect time and way. Accepting delays as part of God's plan and reminding ourselves He has not abandoned us will enable us to serve Him through the delay, as Joseph did.

As I waited to mature in my faith, I held on to my dream of teaching for Him. I accepted opportunities to substitute for more experienced teachers and learned from them. When my children were young, I felt my primary ministry was being their mother, so I faithfully taught them. I took opportunities to teach children's classes and waited for the time when God would use me to teach adults.

Joseph may not have known his servitude was a part of God's plan, but he saw God was with him through it. Others saw it too, especially Potiphar. "The LORD was with Joseph so that he prospered, and he lived in the house of his Egyptian master. When his master saw that the LORD was with him and that the LORD gave him success in everything he did, Joseph found favor in his eyes and became his attendant. Potiphar put him in charge of his household, and he entrusted to his care everything he owned" (Genesis 39:2-4).

Joseph was in the training phase of his God-given dream. The first words of Genesis 39:2, "The LORD was with Joseph," are vital to our understanding of God's dealings with Joseph. Joseph had been taken from his family, stripped of his coat, and snatched from his homeland, but God was with him. God had him exactly where He wanted him.

When our dreams are delayed, the most important thing to remember is God knows exactly where we are. We may even be exactly where He wants us. Regardless of whether we have strayed or God has orchestrated the divergence, God is with us. He has promised, "Never will I leave you; never will I forsake you" (Hebrews 13:5). If we feel God has abandoned us, we are looking in the wrong direction.

God was with Joseph in the pit and in Potiphar's house. As we will see, He will remain with Joseph in the prison and the palace. Wherever Joseph was, he remembered his God and served Him faithfully. In response, God continued to protect Joseph and pour His favor upon him.

During delays, we can remember God is always with us and working toward the dreams He has given us. We can choose to live in the present in His presence. We can trust God will fulfill His plan for our lives if we continue to serve Him even when the situation is bleak.

Joseph continued to serve God as he served others. His current position was all part of God's master plan. Whether he knew it, God placed Joseph in Potiphar's house to teach him the skills he needed to rule the nation. Because he remained faithful, every situation became an opportunity for growth.

We gain much from our delays by considering them to be learning opportunities. If we act like Joseph and serve God faithfully wherever we are, our waiting period will be a time of growth. God uses delays and detours to test our character. He prepares us for future assignments as we serve faithfully in the current ones. We can trust that God is working through the delay to build our character and give us the skills necessary to live our dreams.

One of the first skills Joseph needed was the ability to communicate. He probably spoke Hebrew when he entered Potiphar's house. As he served, he learned to understand and speak the Egyptian language. Since Potiphar was a government official, Joseph may have gained some knowledge of the structure of the Egyptian government and developed an appreciation for the customs of the land. He also learned management skills as he oversaw Potiphar's estate.

On my dream journey, I learned study skills and lesson preparation by teaching children's classes. As I wrote articles for magazines, I gained an understanding of the structure and flow of writing. A well-established ministry invited me to teach three years ago. Its leader mentored me, equipping me with skills to pursue my dream. As I wrote this book, I learned to meet deadlines. I would've loved to jump into my dream earlier, but God knew I needed to learn many skills, so He delayed my dream and presented opportunities for me to grow. He also gave me many victories along the way that kept me motivated to continue.

God gave Joseph success as he served. Joseph's faithfulness caused him to be a blessing to others. Potiphar recognized this and promoted him. "From the time he put him in charge of his household and of all that he owned, the LORD blessed the household of the Egyptian because of Joseph. The blessing of the LORD was on everything Potiphar had, both in the house and in the field" (Genesis 39:5).

When we learn to view detours as an occasion to serve others, we realize every step toward our dreams is an opportunity to bless someone. By choosing to bless others, we become a blessing. God may then entrust us with greater opportunities. "Whoever can be trusted with very little can also be trusted with much" (Luke 16:10). When we take full advantage of every opportunity, we bless Jesus as we bless others.

> When the Son of Man comes in his glory... he will separate the people one from another... Then the King will say to those on his right, "Come, you who are blessed by my Father; take your inheritance, the kingdom prepared for you since the creation of the

world. For I was hungry and you gave me something to eat, I was thirsty and you gave me something to drink, I was a stranger and you invited me in, I needed clothes and you clothed me, I was sick and you looked after me, I was in prison and you came to visit me."

Then the righteous will answer him, "Lord, when did we see you hungry and feed you, or thirsty and give you something to drink? When did we see you a stranger and invite you in, or needing clothes and clothe you? When did we see you sick or in prison and go to visit you?"

The King will reply, "Truly I tell you, whatever you did for one of the least of these brothers and sisters of mine, you did for me." (Matthew 25:31-40)

What we do for others, we're doing for Jesus. He wants to bless them through us. Focusing on the people we bless with our dreams more than the dreams themselves will cause us to live like Jesus. He always showed care and concern for others, and He expects us to do the same. As we view every situation, good or bad, as an opportunity to bless others, we become the hands and feet of Jesus. We can show His love and care for them. This is what dreams are all about. God gives us our dreams to make His dreams come true. He wants everyone to know Him. Through living our dreams, we can introduce others to the God we serve.

There have been stops along my dream path that looked nothing like my dream of writing for God. While raising my own children, I ran an in-home daycare caring for other children. During one season of my life, I worked with the color guard of our local high school band. I've homeschooled other children, watched others' pets, and cleaned houses for extra income. While none of these were consistent with my

God-given dream, they were all opportunities to serve and bless others. By having the right attitude, I could serve Jesus and be an example of Him to them.

We can trust God to give us all the time, energy, and skills we need to do whatever He leads us to do. As we faithfully obey each step, we fulfill His mission. He expects us to share all He gives us generously with others. When we view delays as detours and new opportunities to bless others, God will encourage us and give us the strength to continue our journey. "A generous person will prosper; whoever refreshes others will be refreshed" (Proverbs 11:25).

As we obediently serve God, our dreams become realities, and we develop the skills to take on more responsibility and opportunities to positively impact our world for God. When we have learned those skills, God will take us a step further. This may look like a promotion, as it did when Potiphar placed Joseph over all his possessions, or a demotion, as it did when his brothers sold him into slavery. Reminding ourselves that God is in complete control of our lives, we can assure ourselves that wherever we are is the next step toward our dreams.

With faithfulness, delays become opportunities, and opportunities become responsibilities. Luke 12:48 says, "From everyone who has been given much, much will be demanded; and from the one who has been entrusted with much, much more will be asked." God has entrusted us with dreams and expects us to use them to advance His kingdom. When we remember our dreams are to serve and glorify Him, we will view all circumstances as opportunities, not hindrances.

Our responsibility is to serve God wherever He places us. We can choose to be faithful, focusing on Him and the work He assigns us. First Corinthians 4:2 declares, "It is required that those who have been given a trust must prove faithful." Let's strive to be faithful in all we do for God.

That's what Joseph did, and God showed him favor and blessed all who were under his care. Joseph's exemplary management was rewarded with exceptional trust. "So Potiphar left everything he had in Joseph's care; with Joseph in charge, he did not concern himself with anything except the food he ate" (Genesis 39:6).

Joseph didn't let what seemed to be the death of his dream dissuade him from serving God. Even though he was not where he dreamed of being, he served with integrity and used every opportunity to glorify God. When our paths veer in the wrong direction, we can remind ourselves that following God always leads us in the right direction.

Every pause along our path is an opportunity to serve God by continuing to do what He instructs. We aren't responsible for making our dreams happen. Our responsibility is to serve Him obediently. "So you also, when you have done everything you were told to do, should say, 'We are unworthy servants; we have only done our duty'" (Luke 17:10).

Hard situations often teach integrity. Joseph showed integrity at a young age when he brought a report of his brothers to Jacob (Genesis 37:2). In doing so, he looked out for the interest of his Father. Joseph also served Potiphar with the same integrity.

As we walk along our dream paths, with all their twists and turns, integrity will keep us grounded. Serving God faithfully in every opportunity, planned or unplanned, will help us keep our dreams alive. We can encourage ourselves by saying, "This is just a step toward the dream." Like Jacob who kept Joseph's dream in mind (Gen 37:11) and Mary who "treasured up all these things" occurring at the birth of Jesus "and pondered them in her heart" (Luke 2:19), we can remember the dream and expect God to fulfill it when the time is right.

Regardless of where you are along your dream path, will you determine today to serve Him faithfully in every detour or delay?

Dream Notes:

- Many dreamers experience a delay between recognizing and realizing their dreams.
- Our dream paths may be long, winding, steep, and rocky, but God-given dreams never die.
- We can trust God to fulfill all God-given dreams in His perfect time and way.
- When our dreams are delayed, God knows where we are, and we might be in the exact place He wants us.
- God is always with us and working toward the fulfillment of our God-given dreams even when the situation is bleak.
- God often builds our character and integrity through dream delays which keep us grounded on our dream paths.
- When we view delays as learning opportunities, they become opportunities for growth.

- Every step toward our dreams is an opportunity to bless someone and introduce them to Jesus.
- With faithfulness, delays become opportunities, and opportunities become responsibilities.
- God will give us all the time, energy, and skills we need to do whatever He leads us to do.
- As we faithfully obey God, He fulfills His mission and makes our dreams become realities.

Dream Work:

- How long have you been on your dream path?
- What delays have you faced in achieving your dream?
- How would you describe your current position on your path?
- How can you serve God where you are?
- Who can you bless as you serve in your current situation?
- What might God be teaching you during this time?
- List some challenges you've faced on your dream path. How did you overcome them?

Chapter 6
Temptation Threatens the Dream

Faithfulness does not guarantee adversity won't come. It probably encourages it. Satan cannot stand for us to prosper in any area. Even when our dreams appear dead, he comes against us and tries to prevent us from experiencing the goodness of God. In the depths of delay, we can fight discouragement by anticipating the enemy's attack.

Satan must have hated Joseph prospering in Potiphar's house and God blessing him. He wanted to prevent Potiphar and the other Egyptians from recognizing Joseph served the true God. Satan enacted a plan in Joseph's life to stop the favor and exaltation. "Now Joseph was well-built and handsome, and after a while his master's wife took notice of Joseph and said, 'Come to bed with me!'" (Genesis 39:6-7).

Look how sneaky Satan was. He tried to use what God had given Joseph against him. God creating Joseph handsome, paired with the favor God had poured upon him, made Joseph desirable in the eyes of Potiphar's wife. Not knowing Joseph cared more about serving God than enjoying the pleasures of this world, she attempted to seduce him into her bed.

This reminds us to be careful not to fall for the enemy's ploys to compromise our standards. Joseph could have thought God had abandoned him to slavery and taken the opportunity to experience whatever pleasure he could. But he remembered his God, trusted Him, and continued to serve Him even in trying circumstances.

Joseph refused the wife's advances and asserted, "With me in charge … my master does not concern himself with anything in the house; everything he owns he has entrusted to my care. No one is greater in this house than I am. My master has withheld nothing from me except you, because you are his wife. How then could I do such a wicked thing and sin against God?" (Genesis 39:8-9).

Joseph understood the great trust Potiphar and God had placed in him. He called Potiphar his master, but his true Master was God. He knew he was where he was because of God. It was God who had favored him and blessed him, and it was God who had caused Potiphar to see it and promote him. He knew it would be a wicked thing and a sin against God to sleep with Potiphar's wife, so he continued to resist temptation. "And though she spoke to Joseph day after day, he refused to go to bed with her or even be with her" (Genesis 39:10).

Satan doesn't give up easily, nor should we. We can decide today to continue doing things God's way, regardless of the temptation we face. We can trust He is always working through us and will bless us in every season.

When I faced delays along my dream path, I had to guard against the discouragement of thinking I might never speak or write a book. I resisted the temptation to force my dream into reality. I needed to trust God's plan, see delays as opportunities, and serve Him faithfully wherever He placed me.

Potiphar's wife may have been a beautiful woman who came from wealth and high status herself. As the wife of the captain of the guard, she probably ran in high circles. She might also have been lonely. Maybe Potiphar's job consumed his time. Whether or not these things are true, one thing we know – she set her eyes on Joseph, and she did not intend to give up until she had him. After days, maybe weeks, of being rejected, she made her final play to get the prize she sought.

"One day he went into the house to attend to his duties, and none of the household servants was inside. She caught him by his cloak and said, 'Come to bed with me!' But he left his cloak in her hand and ran out of the house" (Genesis 39:11-12). Joseph had already refused her and said he would not commit evil against Potiphar or God. Finally, she grabbed him by his clothes and demanded that Joseph sleep with her. Joseph fled with such intensity that he left his outer garment in her hands.

Temptation is a powerful force. Even living by God's standards doesn't prevent the tempter from coming. Satan had the audacity to tempt Jesus in the wilderness (Matthew 4:1-11). Knowing the tempter would attack His disciples, Jesus taught them to be ready. "Watch and pray so that you will not fall into temptation. The spirit is willing, but the flesh is weak" (Matthew 26:41). He taught them and us to pray, "And lead us not into temptation, but deliver us from the evil one" (Matthew 6:13).

Knowing temptation will come, as it did to Jesus and His disciples, we need to prepare ourselves to fight against it. Understanding First Corinthians 10:13 will help us develop a battle strategy to resist the evil one. "No temptation has overtaken you except what is common to mankind. And God is faithful; he will not let you be tempted beyond what you can bear. But when you are tempted, he will also provide a way out so that you can endure it."

First, realizing we aren't the first people to face temptation can encourage us. Other servants of God have already faced and overcome any temptation we face. Joseph overcame sexual temptation. Abraham resisted the desire to take the best portion of land for himself. He let Lot choose first even though God had given it all to him (Genesis 13). When Daniel was commanded not to pray, he resisted and prayed anyway, knowing it would land him in the lion's den (Daniel 6). Shadrach, Meshach, and Abednego faced the fiery furnace rather than compromise their faith by bowing to the golden image (Daniel 3:13-23).

Next, we can remind ourselves that God is faithful and won't let us be tempted beyond what we are able. God gives us strength and courage to choose His way. He won't abandon us to temptation. Romans 6:11-18 declares we are dead to sin and alive to God. Sin is no longer our master and cannot reign in our bodies. We have been set free from sin so we can live for God. "Thanks be to God! He gives us the victory through our Lord Jesus Christ" (1 Corinthians 15:57).

Finally, we can look for the way of escape God provides and take it. As we just discussed, sin no longer rules us. God has given us a new nature through the gift of the Holy Spirit. As we learn to submit to His leading, we can escape temptation. "In all these things we are more than conquerors through him who loved us" (Romans 8:37). Through Him we can defeat temptation and become overcomers in all things.

Another way to prepare for temptation is to restrain our fleshly desires. James 1:14-15 explains, "But each person is tempted when they are dragged away by their own evil desire and enticed. Then, after desire has conceived, it gives birth to sin; and sin, when it is full-grown, gives birth to death." Through the power of the Holy Spirit, we can learn to address our desires before they give birth to sin.

We can decide we desire to please God. Studying the Word and learning God's ways will prepare us to resist when temptation comes. We can determine to follow God's instructions. If we fail, we can repent and resume striving to live by His standards.

In doing these, we will learn to "Flee the evil desires of youth and pursue righteousness, faith, love and peace, along with those who call on the Lord out of a pure heart," as Second Timothy 2:22 instructs. We can also expect Satan to flee, because James 4:7 promises, "Submit yourselves, then, to God. Resist the devil, and he will flee from you."

Part of living my dream as a wife and mother included not having a full-time job outside the home. Though I sometimes worked odd jobs and part-time positions, money was often tight, and I was tempted to look for permanent, higher-paying jobs. However, each time I prayed about it, God assured me I was doing what He desired, and I could trust Him to provide for the needs of my family.

Joseph resisted Satan when he faced his temptress, but Potiphar's wife wasn't done with Joseph yet. Scorned by his refusal to succumb to her, she devised an evil plan to discredit him.

> When she saw that he had left his cloak in her hand and had run out of the house, she called her household servants. "Look," she said to them, "this

> Hebrew has been brought to us to make sport of us!
> He came in here to sleep with me, but I screamed.
> When he heard me scream for help, he left his cloak
> beside me and ran out of the house." She kept his
> cloak beside her until his master came home. Then
> she told him this story: "That Hebrew slave you
> brought us came to me to make sport of me. But as
> soon as I screamed for help, he left his cloak beside
> me and ran out of the house." (Genesis 39:13-18)

First, she tried to discredit him among his fellow servants. Maybe she was trying to presuppose the idea that Joseph was the tempter, not her, in case Joseph were to inform Potiphar what she had done. She might also have wanted to make Joseph look bad. Notice she calls him "this Hebrew." Joseph may have told his fellow servants about his God and how He required they serve Him alone. This would have been in stark contrast to the polytheism of the Egyptians.

Potiphar's wife had probably noticed Joseph's ethics. It might have even been part of what initially attracted her to him. Joseph's integrity kept him from giving in to her wishes and infuriated her. When he wouldn't give in, she wanted to not only frame him for attempted rape but also discredit him among his fellow servants. Then, when Potiphar came home, she attempted to seal Joseph's fate by reporting the supposed attempt at rape to her husband.

Satan was working behind the scenes in this. I don't think Satan knows what God is up to, but I think he listens to what we say and do. He heard Joseph tell his dreams as a seventeen-year-old and rejoiced when Joseph was thrown in the pit and sold into slavery. He hoped Joseph would deny his God because of the hardship. But Joseph continued to serve God. Frustrated, he needed a new plan to destroy the dreamer and his dreams. So, he used Potiphar's wife.

I used to have the bad habit of saying, "I can't." I'm sure Satan loved hearing me say this. Then one day, I realized I could if God wanted me to. It didn't matter what the task was—I could trust that if God was calling me to it, He would equip me for it. I learned to speak words of faith and encouragement to myself.

Sometimes we need to remind ourselves that Satan doesn't fight fair. He has no mercy or sympathy. He will kick us when we are down, drive the knife deeper, and pour salt in the open wound. Having no boundaries, he will attack sick people, older adults, young people, new Christians, and poor individuals. He doesn't care. If we are struggling, he wants us to struggle more. He is relentless in the intensity of his attacks.

I have a propensity toward depression. The year after my dad died, my mom's health started declining. When she became unable to live by herself, we moved her into our home. As if that were not enough to deal with, my depression medication stopped working, so my doctor prescribed new ones. I went through several different medications because I reacted severely to them. I suffered anxiety, panic attacks, and even suicidal thoughts. Do you think Satan cared, saw my struggle, and backed off? No, he was determined to turn up the heat and do me in if he could.

What affects his attacks is when he sees us striving to follow God, and it makes him attack all the more. But we can continue trusting and serving God, because He is always with us. Don't worry, dreamer. The enemy can't win.

> What, then, shall we say in response to these things? If God is for us, who can be against us? ... No, in all these things we are more than conquerors through him who loved us. For I am convinced that neither death nor life, neither angels nor demons, neither the present nor the future, nor any powers, neither height nor depth, nor anything else in all creation, will be able to separate us from the love of God that is in Christ Jesus our Lord. (Romans 8:31, 37-39)

Satan thought he had Joseph where he wanted him. Potiphar could have had him killed for the offense. If not, surely, Joseph and his dreams would be thrown away in some deep, dark prison to rot away. This appears to be the case. "When his master heard the story his wife told him, saying, 'This is how your slave treated me,' he burned with anger. Joseph's master took him and put him in prison, the place where the king's prisoners were confined" (Genesis 39:19-20).

We do not know whether Potiphar burned with anger toward Joseph or toward his wife because he sensed she was lying. But he had to respond to the allegations, so he had Joseph thrown in prison.

Joseph, once again, stood accused and condemned for something he did not do. His brothers had hated him because he was loved. They had faked his death and sold him into slavery because he dreamed of being used by God. Now, he sat in prison, accused of the crime that had been committed against him. He had lived with integrity and faithfully stewarded all Potiphar had entrusted to him. By rejecting Potiphar's wife, he had refused to overstep his bounds or commit evil against God. Yet, he was punished.

The Bible presents a tall order for us to fulfill in the book of First Peter.

> Dear friends, do not be surprised at the fiery ordeal that has come on you to test you, as though something strange were happening to you. But rejoice in as much as you participate in the sufferings of Christ, so that you may be overjoyed when his glory is revealed. If you are insulted because of the name of Christ, you are blessed, for the Spirit of glory and of God rests on you ... if you suffer as a Christian, do not be ashamed, but praise God that you bear that name. So then, those who suffer according to God's will should commit themselves to their faithful Creator and continue to do good. (1 Peter 4:12-14, 16, 19)

We should not be surprised when the devil or this world comes against us. As they came against Jesus, they will come against us. Peter tells us to rejoice in our trials because we are sharing in the same suffering Christ endured. We may be insulted because we follow Jesus, but we can praise God because we bear His name. Finally, we can commit ourselves to our faithful Creator and continue to do good.

As I suffered through the side effects of medicine which should have been making me better, I needed to do my best to keep my mental state positive. Even though my circumstances were dark, my mom dying amid my health struggle, I needed to continue to praise God. I made myself pray when I wanted to complain and sing praise songs when I wanted to cry. God rewarded these efforts and helped me make it through one of the darkest times of my life.

When the enemy comes to frustrate and kill our dreams, we can choose to remain faithful to God, keep serving Him, and trust Him to direct our paths. No outside force can delay our dreams. God alone can detour them. Any delay He allows is another step in the right direction. Every detour is a new path we must walk to gain the wisdom and strength we need to attain the dream.

Dream Notes:

- Faithfulness to God and His dream does not guarantee adversity won't come.
- Satan cannot stand for us to prosper in any area. He will do all he can to frustrate us.
- Satan doesn't fight fair, but he can't win.
- We can anticipate the enemy's attack, refuse to compromise our standards, encourage ourselves, and continue obeying God through the attacks.
- Temptation is a powerful force that will come, but we can prepare ourselves to fight against it.
- Other servants of God have faced and overcome similar temptations.
- God is faithful and won't let us be tempted beyond what we are able.
- God gives us strength and courage to look for the way of escape and take it.
- Studying the Word and learning God's ways will prepare us to resist when temptation comes.

- When the enemy threatens our dreams, we can choose to please God, remain faithful, keep serving, and trust Him to direct our paths.

Dream Work:

- What temptations are you currently facing? How do you plan to resist them?
- What decisions can you make today to help you resist future compromises?
- How have you experienced the enemy's relentless attacks?
- How will you continue to fight when the battle gets tough?
- How can you practice rejoicing in suffering?
- In your dream journal, write a statement of faith that you believe God is always in control.
- Add a prayer asking Him to help you rejoice in suffering and remain faithful in every situation.

Chapter 7
Faithful to the Current Dream

So far, we have seen Joseph faithfully serving his father. His brothers hated him, stripped the special robe from his body, threw him in a pit, and sold him into slavery. As a slave in Potiphar's house, Joseph served faithfully. Potiphar promoted him to the head of the household and entrusted everything to him. Unfortunately for Joseph, Potiphar's wife took a liking to him. She tempted him day after day to sleep with her. When Joseph resisted her, she accused him of attempted rape, and Potiphar had Joseph thrown in prison.

We may see similar patterns on our dream paths. There are times we flourish and move toward the dream. Other times, we struggle to trudge forward but often fall back. It might help us to remember this is God's dream. He is the One who gives the dream and determines its fulfillment. God may even give us side dreams along the way.

I've lived several dreams. When I was a child, my dream was to be a wife and a mother. God fulfilled this dream early when I was married at nineteen and had three kids between the ages of twenty-three and thirty. I considered it a blessing to focus on this dream while working side jobs. Then I began dreaming of speaking to women, but God took me down the side path of teaching children and youth. In every place He took me, I tried to live the current dream and learn the lessons He was teaching.

Even when our dreams are delayed, we can choose to be faithful in the current dream. Joseph never dreamed of leaving home or being a slave in a foreign land, yet he served faithfully where God placed him. He willingly lived the current dream, whether it mirrored his original dream.

Remembering God is more important than our dreams will help us when we take detours. Any dream is important because it's an opportunity to serve Him and bring Him glory. Every side path is an opportunity to know God better and show Him to others. God was not only growing Joseph to fulfill his mission but also revealing Himself to Joseph so Joseph could reveal Him to others.

One way we reveal God to those around us is in the way we live. Living righteously in this sinful world shines a light on who God is and what He is like. Christians are called to live differently so others may meet God. "But just as he who called you is holy, so be holy in all you do" (1 Peter 1:15).

Joseph served his father faithfully by bringing him a report of his brothers (Genesis 37:2). The report may have made his brothers mad, but they saw Joseph was truthful. Joseph served faithfully in Potiphar's house by looking over all Potiphar had with such care Potiphar "did not concern himself with anything except the food he ate" (Genesis 39:6). Potiphar, being one of Pharaoh's officials, was probably wealthy and had many servants, who were foreigners or poor Egyptians. He may have had children. All who lived and worked in the house could observe how Joseph served.

Others are watching to see how we live. They notice how we respond in positive and negative situations. As I served in my home, my husband and kids were watching. At church, my words and actions affected other believers. Even in public, as I shopped for groceries and went to doctor's appointments, unbelievers observed my attitude and actions.

We can live in such a way as to bring others closer to God when we develop the attitude Paul had when he said to the Corinthian church, "This, then, is how you ought to regard us: as servants of Christ and as those entrusted with the mysteries God has revealed. Now it is required that those who have been given a trust must prove faithful" (1 Corinthians 4:1-2).

When we regard ourselves as servants of Christ, we can serve faithfully in every situation. Masters entrust their goods to their servants. As servants of God, we have been entrusted with His riches. In First Corinthians 4:1, Paul says we have been put in charge of the 'mysteries of God.' The mystery of salvation through faith in Christ has been revealed to us and is being revealed through us. God has granted us the privilege of revealing to others what He has done to bring them salvation. What we do with this privilege is of grave importance to us and to those God wants to reach through us.

Therefore, Paul calls us to be faithful with the trust God gives us. When we faithfully proclaim the mystery of salvation through our actions and words, others receive the opportunity to become part of God's family. May we live faithful lives as we live our God-given dreams.

Notice the last few words of the verse — "must prove faithful." While every believer has knowledge of salvation and is called to tell others, these words suggest the degree of our faithfulness determines the extent of our opportunities to share with others. The idea of being proven faithful suggests God is watching to see if we're faithfully using the opportunities we have before He advances us toward our dreams.

With Joseph, God gave him multiple opportunities to prove himself faithful–as a son and brother, a shepherd to his father's flock, a slave and steward in Potiphar's house, and now in prison. Each of these served as an occasion for him to prove himself faithful, which he did. God was testing to ensure Joseph would be faithful for the ultimate task of ruling over the storehouses of Egypt.

God does the same with us. He leads us through circumstances to test our faithfulness. He is watching to see if we will be faithful in one area before He advances us to the next opportunity. As He guides us through these, He is training us to be trustworthy and preparing us for more responsibility. How we relate to those around us shows whether we are learning to be faithful stewards of what God entrust to us.

Our circumstances should not affect our service. When we're serving under others, we can follow the instructions of Colossians 3:23-24, "Whatever you do, work at it with all your heart, as working for the Lord, not for human masters, since you know that you will receive an inheritance from the Lord as a reward. It is the Lord Christ you are serving." Since God is our true Master, we can serve heartily regardless of whom we serve under. If we oversee others, we are to remind ourselves that God is our Master and treat those under us "with what is right and fair, because you know that you also have a Master in heaven" (Colossians 4:1).

We can choose to serve our Master anywhere He allows us to be. Joseph's next stop on his dream path was prison. Would he continue to serve God faithfully as he had as a son in his father's house and a slave in Potiphar's?

> But while Joseph was there in the prison, the Lord was with him; he showed him kindness and granted him favor in the eyes of the prison warden. So the warden put Joseph in charge of all those held in the prison, and he was made responsible for all that was done there. The warden paid no attention to anything under Joseph's care, because the Lord was with Joseph and gave him success in whatever he did. (Genesis 39:20-23)

Twice in these verses, we're told, "The Lord was with Joseph." Wherever we are, God is with us. We may find ourselves in situations contrary to the plan we held for our lives. Our dreams may seem dead or delayed, but we're never separated from our Savior. Jesus promised, "Surely I am with you always, to the very end of the age" (Matthew 28:20). Deuteronomy 31:8 assures us, "The LORD himself goes before you and will be with you; he will never leave you nor forsake you. Do not be afraid; do not be discouraged."

When God is with us, our circumstances will not define us. His favor will. Believe the words of our Dream-giver, "So do not fear, for I am with you; do not be dismayed, for I am your God. I will strengthen you and help you; I will uphold you with my righteous right hand" (Isaiah 41:10). Just as God granted Joseph kindness and gave him favor with the prison guard, He will show us the kindness and favor we need to advance wherever we serve.

Prisons nor suffering can stop our dreams. Jesus encouraged the church in Smyrna, "Do not be afraid of what you are about to suffer. I tell you, the devil will put some of you in prison to test you, and you will suffer persecution for ten days. Be faithful, even to the point of death, and I will give you life as your victor's crown" (Revelation 2:10). Even facing prison time, we are to be faithful to our Lord. If it costs us our lives, we are to be faithful, knowing we will receive the victor's crown of life from Him. We can continue to move forward, trusting our Dream-giver with every step we take.

Paul and Silas trusted God throughout their prison experience. They were severely beaten, thrown into prison, and chained by their feet in the inner cell. Around midnight, they were praying and singing hymns to God as the other prisoners listened. "Suddenly there was such a violent earthquake that the foundations of the prison were shaken. At once all the prison doors flew open, and everyone's chains came loose" (Acts 16:23-26).

Paul and Silas refused to let prison keep them from praising God. Even after they were severely beaten, they rejoiced until midnight. God heard them and responded by shaking the prison until the doors flew open. No prison can hold the one God intends to set free, but Paul and Silas did not flee.

When the jailer woke up and saw the prison doors open, he intended to fall upon his sword. Paul shouted to him not to harm himself. The jailer called for lights, rushed in, and saw the prisoners were all there. He fell trembling before Paul and Silas and asked what he must do to be saved. They explained to him, "Believe in the Lord Jesus, and you will be saved." The jailer took them to his house, and "was filled with joy because he had come to believe in God—he and his whole household" (Acts 16:27-34).

Because Paul and Silas didn't let their circumstances, even prison, keep them from worshiping and serving God, the jailer and his household heard the gospel and accepted salvation. If Paul and Silas fled when the doors opened, who would've told the jailer about Jesus? If they complained or cursed those who tortured them, would the jailor have been as likely to listen to their witness?

When we choose to live above our circumstances and continue praising and serving God through the bad times, He will use us to reach others. No prison Satan designs can hold us back or stop the dreams God instills in us. If we find ourselves in prison as Joseph did, may God use us among the prisoners. May He cause the jailers to recognize His power in us and desire to be in relationship with God.

One thing can help us continue to serve God when we feel bound by circumstances is to remember all He has done for us. First Samuel 12:24, reminds us to "serve him faithfully with all your heart; consider what great things he has done for you." When we suffer bad times, we should not forget the good. God has blessed us in so many ways. Recounting those ways can help us stay faithful to Him. He has given us life through His Son. Each day, He wakes us with breath in our lungs. He created this beautiful world for us to live in with all the resources we need for life. "And my God will meet all your needs according to the riches of his glory in Christ Jesus" (Philippians 4:19).

Do you feel bound by circumstances in your life? Are you in a season that seems like a prison?

Early in my stay-at-home mom years, I felt a little like a prisoner in my own home. It may seem silly, but one highlight of my day was going to the mailbox. During a long bout with depression and anxiety, I felt like a prisoner of my mind, constantly fighting to combat the dark thoughts but never seeming to gain complete victory. I have a friend who suffers from a chronic illness and often feels like a prisoner in her home.

In any scenario where we feel trapped, we can strive to serve God faithfully. He has a plan for us in all situations. In my home, I was serving my family. When I was depressed, I tried to connect with and encourage others who were struggling. My friend may feel trapped in her home, but she ministers through the internet and telephone.

We can choose to follow the instructions of Colossians 3:17, "And whatever you do, whether in word or deed, do it all in the name of the Lord Jesus, giving thanks to God the Father through him." An attitude of doing all things in the name of Jesus will ensure we reflect Him properly. Jesus never complained, showed irritation, or impatience. His focus was on caring for those around Him. When we serve with a similar attitude, we will give thanks to God for every opportunity, even the ones contrary to our dreams. Living the current dream with faithfulness propels us forward to our God-given dreams.

Dream Notes:

- God may give us side dreams along our dream paths.

- We can choose to be faithful in the current dream as we struggle to advance on our dream paths.

- God is more important than our dreams.

- Every side path is an opportunity to know God better and reveal Him to others.

- God leads us through circumstances to test our faithfulness and will advance us to the next opportunity when we are ready.

- Since we are defined by God's favor, not our circumstances, we can continue to serve our Master in every situation.

- We can choose to live above our circumstances and continue praising and serving God through every circumstance.

- We can be faithful and continue to move forward, trusting our Dream-giver with every step along our path

- Living the current dream with faithfulness propels us forward to the fulfillment of our God-given dreams.

Dream Work:

- What current dream are you living?

- How might God be using this dream to prepare you for your God-given dream?

- How can you be faithful to God in your current situation? To whom might you reveal the mysteries of salvation?

- Is there any area of your life that feels like a prison? If so, what attitude will you develop to remain faithful through it?

- Can you see a pattern of God moving you forward as you prove yourself faithful in each opportunity, He has given you?
- Ask God to teach you to do all things in the "name of the Lord Jesus."
- Express thankfulness to God for all He has given you.

Chapter 8
Dreams Belong to God

We have seen Joseph survive the pit and Potiphar's house to wind up in prison. Undeterred by the enemy's attack, Joseph continued to serve God faithfully in every situation. God blessed Joseph's faithfulness by giving him favor with the prison guard, and he was put in charge of his fellow prisoners. Although Joseph wasn't living his original dream, we saw he chose to live each day as if it were his dream.

Living for God is less about the dream, and more about glorifying Him. We may not understand how our current circumstances are pushing us toward our dreams, but we can hold on to our Dream-giver by serving Him faithfully wherever we are. Focusing on the now, like Joseph did, is what it takes to see our God-given dreams come true.

In this chapter, we will see Joseph used to help others understand their dreams. We understand Joseph was right where God needed him. The prison was just another pit-stop on the path to the fulfillment of Joseph's God-given dream.

We left Joseph in prison, but not just any prison. This was "the place where the king's prisoners were confined" (Genesis 39:20). God had Joseph exactly where He needed him for the dream to advance.

Have you ever been where you didn't want to be, but later found you were exactly where God wanted you to be? I have. Several years ago, another mother asked me to help homeschool her kids. I really didn't want to, but as my husband and I prayed, we sensed God wanted me to accept her offer. Doing so gave me some spending money, but it also allowed me to be a blessing to her and her kids.

When we find ourselves in trying circumstances, we can remind ourselves God knows where we are. Even if we have caused ourselves to be in the position by taking a wrong turn on our dream paths, God is still in control. He can use it as the next step in our dream process. God will even use Joseph's prison experience to advance the dream.

While Joseph was serving as the overseer of his fellow inmates, two people who will help to advance his dream join him. The king became angry with his chief cupbearer and chief baker and placed them in the same prison where Joseph was, and Joseph was placed in charge of them. After some time, both the cupbearer and the baker dreamed. "Each dream had a meaning of its own" (Genesis 40:1-5).

God was orchestrating the events which would take Joseph from the prison to the palace. He caused these men to be thrown in prison at this time and placed under Joseph's care.

God places people in our lives who will help move us toward our dreams. In my dream of teaching, He has placed me under teachers who helped me learn to teach the Word. He also placed me in one church where the pastor's wife dreamed of having a women's ministry but didn't want to be the primary teacher. We were both excited when she asked me how I would like to serve in the church, and I shared with her my dream of teaching ladies. Together, we started the women's ministry, with me teaching and her organizing. God places us with others, sometimes to advance our dreams, sometimes theirs, and sometimes both.

God sovereignly placed the cupbearer and baker in Joseph's prison and caused them to dream on the same night. The next morning, Joseph noticed they both looked disheartened and inquired why. They reveal they have both dreamed dreams, and they were sad because there was no one to interpret the dreams to them (Genesis 40:6-8).

Joseph cared about those around and under him. He could have become bitter and hardhearted through his trials, believed his suffering surpassed that of others, and felt no empathy for them. Instead, he cared enough to ask what was bothering them. All the detours did not discourage him. He remained committed to serving God faithfully wherever he was.

We can't control our circumstances, but we can control how we respond to them. The Apostle Paul faced extreme circumstances. He worked hard, but was in prison frequently, had been flogged severely, and was exposed to death many times. Five times he received forty lashes minus one; three times he was beaten with rods; and once he was pelted with stones. Having been shipwrecked three times, he spent a night and a day in the open sea. He was constantly on the move and faced dangers from rivers, bandits, Jews, Gentiles, and false believers. He was in danger in the city, the country, and at sea. He labored and toiled, went without sleep, suffered hunger, thirst, cold, and nakedness (2 Corinthians 11:23-27). Yet, he continued to serve the Lord by preaching the gospel because he cared about lost souls.

When Joseph heard the cupbearer and baker were sad because there was no interpretation to their dreams, he encouraged them by pointing them to God. Joseph said to them, "Do not interpretations belong to God?" (Genesis 40:8).

These are words of great faith spoken by a man who had seen his dream snatched from him. Despite discouraging circumstances, he continued to point others to his faithful God. By now, many would have probably given up on their dreams, but not Joseph. He still trusted God controlled his life and credited Him as the giver and interpreter of dreams. Joseph still believed his dream was from God. Despite struggling to understand how God could fulfill it, he did not give up on the Dream-giver.

The interpretations of our dreams also belong to God. Our dreams may appear one way to us, but their fulfillment may be a whole different story. It's very possible to misinterpret the meaning of the dreams God gives us. For this reason, it's important to trust God more than we trust the dream. Life is about living for God, not just living the dream. If we faithfully serve Him despite our circumstances, as Joseph did, we will come to the end of whatever He has planned for us.

I had a friend who dreamed of buying a house and turning it into a home for struggling teen girls. She didn't realize her dream in that way. Chronic health issues caused her to spend much of her time secluded at home. But God has a way of making dreams come true even when our lives hinder them. My friend's dream came true through her computer. As she sat in her home, she connected with and ministered to young women all over the country through the internet.

Joseph saw his dream of rising above his family ripped from him as the coat of many colors was ripped from his body. Maybe he then decided his dream meant he would be the head servant in Potiphar's house, so he resigned to serve God there. This dream was also ripped from him as his cloak was ripped from his body by Potiphar's wife. But he continued to trust God. Even in the prison, he served his Dream-giver. By the time he landed in prison and heard the dreams of the cupbearer and the baker, he had learned all too well "interpretations belong to God."

The same is true of our dreams. There may appear to be a large discrepancy between what we think they mean and how they play out. While Joseph interpreted his dream correctly, circumstances appeared otherwise. Yet, he still served. We do well to continue serving God wherever circumstances lead us. When we serve faithfully in the current dream, we can trust God is preparing us for the fulfillment of the ultimate dream.

My dream path began with teaching my own children, which led to teaching children's and youth classes. Next, I was teaching adults at my church. Finally, I began teaching at other churches, speaking at conferences and retreats. I learned to write my own lessons. Each of these stops was a dream, and each led to the next step headed to the fulfillment of my ultimate dream, to be a Christian author.

With the cupbearer and the baker, we see some dreams have good interpretations while others have bad. We shouldn't let this discourage us. Since we are children of God, we can know the plans God has for us are always good. The ultimate plan is for us to be with Him in glory. Everything we face on earth leads to this end.

Joseph invited his fellow prisoners to tell him their dreams. The cupbearer began, "In my dream I saw a vine in front of me, and on the vine were three branches. As soon as it budded, it blossomed, and its clusters ripened into grapes. Pharaoh's cup was in my hand, and I took the grapes, squeezed them into Pharaoh's cup and put the cup in his hand" (Genesis 40:9-11).

Joseph interpreted the dream to mean Pharaoh would restore the cupbearer to his former position in three days. The cupbearer must have been pleased. Joseph used this opportunity to address his situation. He asked the cupbearer to remember the kindness he showed and relate to Pharaoh how he was forcibly taken from his homeland, sold into slavery, and thrown into the prison unjustly (Genesis 40:12-15).

When the baker saw the interpretation for the cupbearer was favorable, he eagerly told Joseph his dream. "I too had a dream: On my head were three baskets of bread. In the top basket were all kinds of baked goods for Pharaoh, but the birds were eating them out of the basket on my head." Unfortunately, for the baker, his interpretation was not as favorable. Joseph said his dream would also come true in three days, but instead of being reinstated, Pharaoh would lift off his head, impale his body on a pole, and leave his flesh for the birds (Genesis 40:16-19).

The fulfilment of the cupbearer's and the baker's dreams happened exactly as God revealed they would through Joseph. In three days, the cupbearer was reinstated, and the baker was executed (Genesis 40:20-22).

As we have already seen with Joseph, our dreams may not look exactly as we thought they would. They will, however, be exactly what God planned for them to be. He created us for a purpose. Ephesians

2:10 declares, "For we are God's handiwork, created in Christ Jesus to do good works, which God prepared in advance for us to do." As Christians, we have been created to fulfill His purpose. We can walk confidently through our lives doing the good works He has called us to without fearing negative outcomes.

Our ultimate good work is to glorify our heavenly Father. We do this as we live like Joseph, faithfully serving Him. Whether we know our dreams, question their interpretation, or reason our dreams are dead, we are to serve Him. How God glorifies Himself through us is up to Him. We are to serve and obey Him whether we are in the pit, Potiphar's house, or the prison. We can trust Him to complete His mission through us.

Sometimes God will grant us knowledge of what He is doing, other times He will not. Even when we are unsure of our direction, we can trust God leads us to fulfill His dreams for us as we follow Him.

When my husband, Clay, was an upcoming junior in high school, he dreamed of playing football in college. He was offered a football scholarship to play at Eastern Kentucky University but injured his knee the next year. Having lost the scholarship opportunity, he attended college in my hometown. We met, fell in love, married, and had three kids. When Clay lost his scholarship, he didn't know it at the time, but God led him to his dream of having a family.

Joseph had not made it to his dream yet, but he would. He would remain in prison for two more years before his dream advanced. "The chief cupbearer … did not remember Joseph; he forgot him" (Genesis 40:23). Joseph may have felt forgotten by God, but he wasn't.

God never forgets us. When we feel forgotten, we may question whether we have killed our dreams. How badly would we have to mess up to negate our dreams?

The Apostle Peter made many mistakes. He often spoke and did the wrong things. He was the one who warned Jesus not to talk about His coming death (Matthew 16:22) and was the one who cut off the ear of the high priest's servant when they came to arrest Jesus (John 18:10). After Jesus' arrest, Peter denied knowing Him (Matthew 26:69-75). Did these things negate his dream?

Peter moved forward down his God-given path and became a key leader in the early church. He preached the first sermon after Pentecost, and three thousand received salvation (Acts 2:14-41). He continued to preach boldly, perform miracles, and write two New Testament books. Peter's mistakes didn't keep God from using him just as He pleased.

What if our mistakes are worse than Peter's? David was anointed to be king as a young man. He experienced significant victories, including his victory over Goliath, but he also endured many failures. The two most prominent and questionable failures happened after he became king. In the spring, when all the kings went to war, David stayed home. One evening as he stood on the rooftop of his palace, he looked over and saw a beautiful woman bathing. She was so beautiful David sent his servants to find out who she was. When he was informed, she was a married woman named Bathsheba, it did not stop David's lustful plan. He took her into his bed and committed adultery with her against Uriah and his own wives (2 Samuel 11:1-4).

When Bathsheba revealed her pregnancy with David's child, he tried to cover his sin. He tried to trick Uriah into sleeping with Bathsheba, so the child would be considered his. But Uriah refused to be with his wife while his men were at war. David then devised a dastardly plan to have Uriah killed. He sent Uriah back to the front with a letter to one of the military commanders ordering him to lead Uriah into the fiercest part of the battle and then withdraw from him. When the plan was fulfilled, David had committed murder to cover up adultery (2 Samuel 11:14-17).

Even these evil sins did not negate God's plan for David. He committed adultery and murder, but God allowed him to remain as king and continued to use him mightily. Yes, there were consequences–the baby born to Bathsheba died (2 Samuel 12:18). Yet, she continued as David's wife, and God even allowed the next king of Israel, Solomon, to be born through her (2 Samuel 12:24).

Our God specializes in bringing good from bad. We may mess up along our dream paths, sin, or go the wrong way, but God can redeem even our mistakes. Our original question was—How bad would we have to mess up to negate the dreams God designed for us? I would like to suggest we can't mess up badly enough to negate our dreams. If adultery and murder didn't negate David's, our sins won't negate ours. Yes, we may face consequences and discipline for our actions, but when we come back to God in true repentance as David did (2 Samuel 12:13), He will forgive us and move us forward again toward our dreams.

I've messed up many times. Like the Apostle Peter, I often speak before I think. I don't intend to, but sometimes my words seem unkind.

Many times, I've had to ask God to forgive me and go to the person I have spoken to and apologize for my words. I've also made poor decisions by accepting positions God didn't call me to. Other times, I've declined opportunities I later realized were from God. None of these mistakes negated my dream. God even used them to teach me to be more careful about what I say and agree to.

Fellow dreamers, I believe the only way we can stop our dreams is to refuse to live them. I would not expect a refusal from someone who cares enough about his or her dream to read this book. So, let's take whatever mistakes and sins we have committed and place them where they should be, in the hands of our Father. He stands ready to forgive and redeem whatever we confess. He is prepared to move us back onto the right path and head us toward our dreams.

Dream Notes:

- Living for God is less about our dreams and more about glorifying Him.
- All the plans God has for His children are good.
- Our dreams may not look exactly as we thought, but they will be exactly what God planned.
- We can't control our circumstances, but we can control how we respond to them.
- We can trust God, knowing He controls our dreams' interpretations and fulfillment.
- There may be a large discrepancy between what we think our dreams mean and how God fulfills them.

- God will complete His mission through us since He never forgets us or our dreams.

- Our ultimate good work is to glorify God by faithfully serving Him in the current dream as He prepares us for our ultimate dreams.

- God places people in our lives who will help move us toward our dreams.

- While we may face consequences for our mistakes, we can't mess up badly enough to negate our dreams.

- When we repent and begin following God again, He restores us and places us back on our dream paths.

- The only way we can stop our dreams is to refuse to live them.

Dream Work:

- Have you seen discrepancies between what you thought your dream meant and how God is fulfilling them?

- How can you glorify God in your current situation?

- How are you pointing others to God?

- Who has God used to help you move toward your dream?

- Who can you help walk toward their dreams?

- What mistakes have you made along your dream path?

- When have you feared you have forfeited your dream by veering from your dream path?

- If you are currently far from your path, ask God to forgive you and trust He will place you back on the path headed in the right direction.

Chapter 9
Path to the Dream

Two years passed as Joseph waited in prison, hoping the cupbearer would remember him and speak to Pharaoh on his behalf (Genesis 41:1). Two years, and nothing. Again, Joseph's dream was delayed. I imagine Joseph must've wondered what God as up to. Afterall, he faithfully served God despite the setbacks and detours. Like Joseph, when setbacks occur, we're challenged to trust God so that we never give up on our dreams, no matter the circumstance.

Could it be, the bigger the dream, the longer the preparation? God was preparing Joseph to serve as second in command of Egypt, to save all the world from famine, and to bring his family to this foreign land. It's no wonder he needed so much training.

Our paths to our dreams may seem never-ending. But God knows what He is doing. Every delay is carefully designed by Him. He uses each moment to ensure we are fully prepared to receive our dreams. I dreamed of writing long before I received a publishing contract. Looking back, I can see how God used each stop along my journey to grow and prepare me. Each step led me one step closer to the fulfillment of the dream. God's slowness to act was not unconcern. His timing was perfect.

Despite two years of waiting to be exonerated, Joseph was closer to his dream than he could ever imagine. It was now Pharaoh's turn to dream. He dreamed he was standing by the Nile and saw seven fat cows grazing among the reeds. As they did, seven haggard cows rose from the Nile and ate them. This disturbing dream awoke Pharaoh. He fell back asleep and dreamed again. This time he saw seven healthy heads of grain growing on a single stalk. Seven thin, scorched-looking heads of grain sprouted and swallowed them. When Pharaoh woke up the next morning, he was troubled. He consulted the magicians and wise men of Egypt, but no one could interpret his dreams (Genesis 41:1-8).

God giving dreams to this pagan king shows He cares about the entire world and reminds us He is in control of all lands. "In the LORD's hand the king's heart is a stream of water that he channels toward all who please him" (Proverbs 21:1). Trusting God to direct those who rule, we can pray for government officials whether we agree with them. First Timothy 2:1-2 commands, "I urge, then, first of all, that petitions, prayers, intercession and thanksgiving be made for all people—for kings and all those in authority, that we may live peaceful and quiet lives in all godliness and holiness."

Those in authority over us don't control our dreams. God is our authority. He can and will use whoever is above us. Even if our employer is an unbeliever, God can give us favor with them as He did with Joseph in Potiphar's house. He can lead the ungodly to make decisions which support our dreams, just as He did with Pharaoh.

God sending Pharoah the dream about the land reminds us of our dreams are for others. Pharaoh's dream was about the people he governed. God was giving him a warning of the coming famine and directing him so that he could save his people. Likewise, we are to live our dreams to serve others and glorify God. Ephesians 4:12 teaches our spiritual gifts are given "to equip his people for works of service, so that the body of Christ may be built up."

All God-given dreams are for expanding the kingdom. If our careers are the same as our dreams, we can stay God-focused as we work and aim to reveal Christ to those around us. When our families are our priority, we should model Christ and guide them to faith. If our dreams involve serving in a church or ministry, we can accomplish them with God's strength and wisdom.

As I live my dream to write and speak for God, my focus should be ministering to others. I don't live my dream for what I can gain, but for how I can draw others closer to God.

Finally, the cupbearer remembered Joseph. When the chief cupbearer heard about Pharaoh's dreams, he exclaimed, "Today I am reminded of my shortcomings." He told Pharaoh how he and the baker each dreamed while they were in prison and how a young Hebrew revealed the meaning of each. He relayed to Pharaoh all things turned out exactly as Joseph interpreted them. "Pharaoh sent for Joseph, and he was quickly brought from the dungeon. When he had shaved and changed his clothes, he came before Pharaoh" (Genesis 41:9-14).

Have you lived through times you felt forgotten in prison? I have. I lived for years aching to teach with no outlet to do so. When I was asked to lead women's, ministry then have the offer removed, I felt bound as I watched someone else do the job I thought God called me to. Later in the same church, I was given the position. I just needed to wait for God's perfect timing.

When it is time to live our dreams, doors will fly open. I currently serve as a Sunday school teacher and women's ministry leader. Monthly, I teach at a ladies' event in another town, and yearly at a conference run by the same ministry. I also speak at churches in my area at special events. In fact, I've turned some down because of previously scheduled events. I share all of this to show what God can do. It seemed like God said, "Okay, I'm ready to use you. See if you can keep up."

Joseph prepared to meet the king. God prepares us to meet those who can advance our dreams. He opens doors we don't even know exist. Billie Corley runs the ministry in which I work. I met Billie at the first writer's conference I ever attended. Years later we reconnected, and she invited me to join her ministry team. In working with her, I met my current publisher. How would I have known the connections God planned through one conference? But God knows what He is doing. He leads us to and gives us favor with the people who will help make our dreams come true.

Joseph was about to meet the person God would use to advance his God-given dream. Pharaoh explained to Joseph he had dreams no one could interpret, but he heard Joseph could do so. Joseph answered, "I cannot do it … but God will give Pharaoh the answer he desires" (Genesis 41:15-16).

Joseph was very careful not to take credit for dream interpretation. He said, God would give the answer. God deserves all the credit in everything we do. He is the one who gives us abilities and opportunities. "Not that we are competent in ourselves to claim anything for ourselves, but our competence comes from God" (2 Corinthians 3:5).

I mentioned all the ministry opportunities God is currently giving me. It has been a delightful roller coaster that has left my head spinning. Through it all, God has been faithful. When I was feeling overwhelmed by all the work it entails, I expressed to Him, "If You want me to do it, then You're going to have to do it through me," and He has. He is teaching me the meaning of Second Corinthians 9:8 which says, "And God is able to bless you abundantly, so that in all things at all times, having all that you need, you will abound in every good work."

We serve a God who is unlimited in His ability to bless. All resources are at His disposal to do with them as He pleases. He is not a stingy God, but One who loves blessing His children. He is able and willing to bless us abundantly so we will fulfill the dreams He has given us. According to Second Corinthians 9:8, we have all we need to do all the good work He has planned at all times and in all things. We can confidently expect God to supply whatever we need for our dreams to come true.

Joseph declared, "Interpretations belong to God." He knew God would have to tell him what the dreams meant, and he trusted God to do so.

I've realized it's God who teaches, speaks, and writes through me. If not for Him, I wouldn't even be able to utter one word, and I certainly wouldn't be able to explain His. If I forget this and try to teach on my own, He may let me. However, without His power, my words will not produce spiritual fruit. I need Him every moment of every day in every task.

Pharaoh related his dreams about the cows and heads of grain. Joseph explained to Pharaoh both dreams had the same meaning, and God was revealing to Pharaoh what He was about to do. Both the seven good cows and the seven good heads of grain represented seven years of plenty in the land. Likewise, the seven lean cows and the seven worthless heads of grain represented seven years of famine. Joseph said God was revealing to Pharaoh there would be seven years of great abundance in Egypt followed by seven years of famine so severe the people would forget the previous abundance. God gave Pharaoh the dream in two forms to show the coming famine was certain and would happen soon (Genesis 41:17-33).

Then Joseph bravely advised Pharaoh what to do in response to the dream. Pharaoh didn't ask for advice, but God's Spirit empowered Joseph to give Pharaoh the instructions he needed to save his people.

When God gives us direction, we are to step forward boldly however He directs, trusting He knows and controls the plan. We may have to take bold, uncomfortable steps to advance our dreams. Although I am a teacher and a speaker, I hate to be the center of attention. Seeing it's almost impossible to present a lesson without others paying attention to you, I needed to learn to be comfortable in the spotlight. I learned the lesson really wasn't about me–it was about God. I learned to feel more comfortable by remembering I was shining the light on Him, not on myself.

Joseph advised Pharaoh,

Now let Pharaoh look for a discerning and wise man and put him in charge of the land of Egypt. Let

Pharaoh appoint commissioners over the land to take a fifth of the harvest of Egypt during the seven years of abundance. They should collect all the food of these good years that are coming and store up the grain under the authority of Pharaoh, to be kept in the cities for food. This food should be held in reserve for the country, to be used during the seven years of famine that will come upon Egypt, so that the country may not be ruined by the famine. (Genesis 41:33-36)

Joseph's plan appeared wise to Pharaoh, and he discerned there was no one wiser in Egypt. Joseph knew what the dream meant, knew what to do about it, and knew the God who sent it. Pharaoh reasoned Joseph must have been the one to enact the plan to save Egypt.

God enables the ones He calls. My former preacher taught that the person who saw a particular need was usually the one God was calling to meet the need. A dream often begins when we see people in need of ministering, and we desire to meet their need. When God leads us to a ministry or position, we can trust He will show us the details as He leads the way.

My friend, who is an exceptional singer, was called upon to lead music at a new church. Having never led music service, she was apprehensive, but God had given her some qualities she needed. She was diligent, organized, and personable. In faith, she stepped into the position, and God grew her as she relied on Him and served. Nine years later, she is still gifting the members of her church with Spirit-led Sunday morning worship.

Joseph's plan sounded good to Pharaoh and his officials. So, Pharaoh asked them, "Can we find anyone like this man, one in whom is the spirit of God?" Pharaoh acknowledged God made these things known to Joseph and realized there was no one so discerning or wise. He made Joseph second in command putting him in charge of the palace and commanding all his people to submit to Joseph's orders (Genesis 41:37-40).

Finally, Joseph was exalted as a ruler who commanded the affairs of all of Egypt. But this still did not fulfill the original dream. Maybe Joseph thought he misinterpreted his original dream. Even now, how could his family, who were far away, bow down to him? Maybe he reasoned the sheaves of grain and stars represented the people of Egypt. But this was just another step to fulfilling the dream exactly as God intended it to be. God was still setting the stage.

Early in my dream of being a writer, I thought writing my own Sunday school lessons might be what God planned. Now I see it was preparation for learning to write books. Learning to teach a class each week was preparation for teaching in Billie's ministry. It was all a step in the process. I don't know where God is taking me, but I want to be faithful and continue along the journey until I am fully living the dream.

We continue to live our dreams as long as we live. Our mission is never complete until we reach heaven and hear, "Well done, good and faithful servant! You have been faithful with a few things; I will put you in charge of many things. Come and share your master's happiness!" (Matthew 25:23). The goal is to live our lives so we will hear these words.

Focusing on pleasing God each day will ensure He will be pleased with our lives. Each day is a step on the path to the dream. To make it successfully to the end, we must continue taking each step in the direction He instructs. Each day we can ask, "God, did I do well today? Are You pleased?" He will answer by giving us assurance we have, or He will instruct us what to do differently.

We can trust our Dream-giver to be our Dream-leader as we walk the path to our dreams.

Dream Notes:

- The bigger the dream, the longer the preparation.
- Every delay is carefully designed by God to prepare us for our dreams.
- We can trust our Dream-giver to be our Dream-leader as we walk the path to our dreams.
- Those in authority over us don't control our dreams. God does.
- God calls us to use our dreams to minister to others, expand the kingdom, and draw others closer to Him.
- Our mission of bringing others to God is not complete until we reach heaven
- When we feel forgotten, we need to wait for God's perfect timing.
- We can take the bold steps God directs to advance our dreams knowing He controls the plan and will enable us to reach them.
- We can confidently expect God to supply whatever we need for our dreams to come true.
- Focusing on pleasing God each day ensures He will be pleased with our lives.

Dream Work:

- Has there been a time in your life when you felt forgotten?

- Have you discovered how God wants to use your dream to benefit others and glorify Himself?

- What doors is God opening for you along your dream path?

- How have you seen Second Corinthians 9:8 fulfilled in your life? "And God is able to bless you abundantly, so that in all things at all times, having all that you need, you will abound in every good work."

- What bold step of faith is God calling you to take toward your dream?

Chapter 10
Working the Dream

Joseph has come a long way since we first met him. From a child in his father's house to the second in command of Egypt. We might be tempted to think he finally achieved success. While it is true his life was better than it was in the pit or prison, it has cost Joseph a lot to get where he is and he still has a lot of hard work to do.

Living our dreams may be costly. We may have to give time, money, or energy for them. As I've shared, I pursue my dream full time and rely on God to provide for me and my family through my husband's job alone. I also spend a lot of time studying, preparing lessons, and teaching. I travel to other towns to speak at churches. I must be willing to listen and minister to others even when I feel tired or stressed.

Living the dream is not a life of ease. Dream work is hard work. When we come to the fulfillment of our dreams, it is not time to sit back and glory in our accomplishments. It is time to push forward and strive to bring our Dream-giver more glory. We continue to work to produce the fruit that He desires. Jesus said, "This is to my Father's glory, that you bear much fruit" (John 15:8). We are to continue to live the dream by working it and bearing the fruit that it yields. All we give to serve Jesus is worth the benefits of ministering in His name. We can't out give God. When we turn our lives over to Him as Joseph did and serve faithfully wherever He places us, we will experience the joy of living the dreams He has for us.

As I sit typing this chapter, many other commitments sit on my to-do list, including prepping to teach an upcoming class, a blog to edit and publish, a conference to pack for, and a lesson to prepare for a week from now. Each of these are commitments with a deadline, so I prayerfully schedule the time to do each, and trust God will help me complete them.

Joseph probably felt similar pressures. God gave him wisdom to counsel Pharaoh what to do about the coming famine, but he probably didn't expect to be put in charge of the task. He would need to trust God to continue to give him wisdom to handle the affair and be willing to work diligently as he lived this part of his dream.

> So Pharaoh said to Joseph, "I hereby put you in charge of the whole land of Egypt." Then Pharaoh took his signet ring from his finger and put it on Joseph's finger. He dressed him in robes of fine linen and put a gold chain around his neck. He had him ride in a chariot as his second-in-command, and people shouted before him, "Make way!" Thus he put him in charge of the whole land of Egypt. Then Pharaoh said to Joseph, "I am Pharaoh, but without your word no one will lift hand or foot in all Egypt." (Genesis 41:41-44)

Joseph progressed a long way through his troubles. God used each of the challenges to grow him and prepare him for his new assignment in Egypt. Each of the troubles we face has prepared us for the advancement God has planned. As we have seen with Joseph, responding to trouble with integrity teaches us the new skills we need for the next assignment.

I found being a stay-at-home mom challenging. It seemed like there was always something needing to get done and someone who needed me. I did my best, often messed up, but recovered, and moved forward with the next task. Having completed that joyous but difficult season of my life, I can look back and see how God used it to prepare me for my dream. He taught me time management to meet deadlines, patience to deal with others who differ from me, diligence to keep working until a task is done, and resilience to shake off failures and keep pressing forward.

God has already prepared us for the portion of the dream to which He brings us. It serves us well to remember what we have come through and acknowledge it's all because of Him.

Imagine Joseph standing before the people of Egypt wearing the fine linen robe. Do you think it reminded him of the coat of many colors from his father? He had experienced it ripped from his body by ones he dearly loved. Now, he stood exalted, dressed in finery before strangers. On his hand, he wore the signet ring of Pharaoh, which empowered him to control the commerce of the land. He rose from the younger brother who was despised to a man of importance who rode in a fine chariot. No longer despised or seen as less than, he was second-in-command and acknowledged by all.

God did this. There was no way Joseph could have moved to Egypt and asked to be in charge. He would have been laughed at, or worse, executed. But God does the impossible. He can and will advance us to any position He decides, and He often uses some unusual methods to do so.

I have seen my dream advance in strange ways. I already shared about meeting Mrs. Billie years before she invited me to work in her ministry. Another time, God allowed someone else to be given a teaching job I thought He was preparing for me. I accepted His choice but found it strange this person moved within six months of taking the position. Then, I was told I was needed in the position. God has His ways. I don't always understand them, but I'm learning to accept them.

For Joseph, his new position also came with some big changes. Joseph was given a new name, Zaphenath-Paneah, and a wife, Asenath, the daughter of the priest of On. During the seven years of plenty, Joseph and his wife welcomed two sons to their family, named Manasseh and Ephraim. These names represented Joseph forgetting the trouble from his father's house and the fruitfulness God brought through his suffering (Genesis 41:45-46, 50-52).

Joseph flourished as he lived in the land of Egypt, but with much privilege comes much responsibility. Joseph performed the tasks the position of second in command required. Dreamtime is not lazy time. It's a busy time with much activity. Living the dream takes a lot of hard work. For seven years, Joseph labored diligently to do the work appointed to him by God through Pharaoh.

Working in the years of plenty prepares us for the years of famine coming. Proverbs 27:1 warns, "Do not boast about tomorrow, for you do not know what a day may bring." We should not put off until tomorrow what we can do today. We are wise to live our lives, each day, according to the instructions of James 4:13-15, "Now listen, you who say, 'Today or tomorrow we will go to this or that city, spend a year there, carry on business and make money.' Why, you do not even know what will happen tomorrow. What is your life? You are a mist that appears for a little while and then vanishes. Instead, you ought to say, 'If it is the Lord's will, we will live and do this or that.'"

Since we can't predict tomorrow, we can live for today and do the work God gives us now. While our focus in this book is living the dream, I want to make sure we understand living the dream isn't all about working. Joseph had a wife and children. He spent time with them, connecting with his wife and teaching his boys. He was raising two of the future leaders of the twelve tribes of Israel. We shouldn't assume Joseph's life was all work and no enjoyment, but neither was it all enjoyment and no work. Joseph had a lot to do, as do we. We can learn to balance our dream life with our home life if we're to be rightly living the dream God has given us.

We live the dream as we give each day fully to God. "Therefore do not worry about tomorrow, for tomorrow will worry about itself. Each day has enough trouble of its own" (Matthew 6:34). While we should not worry, we are to plan as God leads us each day. Planning today provides for tomorrow. We see this modeled in Joseph's life. He worked each day, performing his assigned task, and completed the job by the end of the seven years of plenty.

When the seven years of abundance ended, seven years began in which there was a famine in all the lands. But in the land of Egypt there was food. When the Egyptians began to suffer, they cried to Pharaoh, and he told them, "Go to Joseph and do what he tells you." Joseph opened the storehouses and sold them the grain he had stored.

Because the famine was severe, people from all lands came to Egypt to buy grain (Genesis 41:53-57).

Joseph and Egypt were prepared because they obeyed God's leading to store up the grain. Not only did they have food for their families, but they also possessed food to sell to the other lands which also suffered from the famine.

When we obey God, He provides for us and prepares us to be a blessing to others. Our talents are never about ourselves. Ephesians 4:12-13 explains God gives us spiritual gifts "to equip his people for works of service, so that the body of Christ may be built up until we all reach unity ... attaining to the whole measure of the fullness of Christ." When we choose to use our God-given gifts to work in our God-given dreams, God uses us to bless other believers and build the body of Christ into the fullness He designed it to be. "Now to each one the manifestation of the Spirit is given for the common good" (1 Corinthians 12:7).

Having been given the gift of teaching, I teach. Because I have the gift of encouragement, I need to strive to encourage others. My husband has the gift of service, so he gladly takes the time to help others with home projects and ministry activities. I have a friend with the gift of administration who coordinates Vacation Bible School at her church. We aim to use our gift to build up other believers as First Peter 4:10-11 instructs us, "Each of you should use whatever gift you have received to serve others, as faithful stewards of God's grace in its various forms ... with the strength God provides, so that in all things God may be praised through Jesus Christ."

Joseph used his gifts in the land of Egypt, and God used him to provide for the Egyptians and his long-lost family. Back in his homeland of Canaan, Joseph's family also suffered from the effects of the famine. Jacob heard there was grain in Egypt and came up with a plan to provide for his family. He called together ten of his sons and told them, "I have heard that there is grain in Egypt. Go down there and buy some for us, so that we may live and not die." All but one brother who remained in Jacob's household went down to Egypt to buy grain. Jacob refused to send Benjamin because he was the only living son of Rachel. He was afraid harm might come to him (Genesis 42:1-5).

Now, we see the ten brothers who sold Joseph into slavery marching toward Egypt, never suspecting they were headed to encounter the one they betrayed. How the tables have turned. Years ago, they held Joseph's future in their hands as they attempted to kill his dream by faking his death. Now, Joseph held their future in his hands, as he was the one they must see to buy grain.

God often has surprising ways of turning the tables. Joseph nor his brothers probably ever suspected one day Joseph would stand before them as second in command of the most powerful nation in the land. Neither could they know their act of sabotage would save them and their whole family from starvation.

We may not know what God is doing, but He is always working behind the scenes, fulfilling His plan, and growing His kingdom. He uses us to advance His plan by giving us dreams and assigning our tasks. When we do our part, we will live the dream and see His come true.

I don't understand why God uses such broken vessels to advance His plan, but He does. Second Corinthians 4:7 declares, "But we have this treasure in jars of clay to show that this all-surpassing power is from God and not from us." We have the treasure of knowing God and being able to share Him. God intends us to be a blessing in doing so.

Our mission will not always be easy. Think of Joseph and all he had endured before he arrived at the position where he could bless his family. Second Corinthians 4:8-9 continues, "We are hard pressed on every side, but not crushed; perplexed, but not in despair; persecuted, but not abandoned; struck down, but not destroyed." Fellow dream walker, do you feel hard-pressed and struck down? Do not despair; we will not be crushed or destroyed. God will never abandon us.

Joseph may have felt abandoned by God, but he was not. God was with him, leading him to the place of his dreams. He is also with us, and we can trust Him to lead us to the fulfillment of His dreams for us.

Paul reminds us, "All this is for your benefit, so that the grace that is reaching more and more people may cause thanksgiving to overflow to the glory of God" (2 Corinthians 4:15). We can choose to suffer all the trying circumstances God allows in our lives, like Joseph did, knowing God is working all things to reach more people. We talked previously about how God used Joseph as a witness of Himself in Potiphar's house. Now, he has been exalted to second in command of Egypt. Might God have placed him there not only to save his family from famine, but to show the Egyptians He was the true God?

Wherever God has placed us, He wants to show Himself through us. Knowing this will help us obey these instructions, "Therefore we do not lose heart. Though outwardly we are wasting away, yet inwardly we are being renewed day by day. For our light and momentary troubles are achieving for us an eternal glory that far outweighs them all. So we fix our eyes not on what is seen, but on what is unseen, since what is seen is temporary, but what is unseen is eternal" (2 Corinthians 4:16-18).

Take heart, dream walker, we're being renewed day by day. One day our heavy troubles of today will seem light and momentary considering all our Dream-giver will accomplish. We can choose to fix our eyes on the eternal, which is Jesus and His mission. We rejoice knowing He is working all things out for our good, the good of others, and His glory.

Dream Notes:
- Living the dream is costly and takes a lot of hard work.
- God can and will advance us to any position He decides.
- He often uses unusual methods to advance our dreams.
- God has already prepared us for the portion of the dream to which He brings us.
- We live the dream as we give each day fully to God and strive to bring Him glory.
- When we obey God, He provides for us and prepares us to be a blessing to others.
- When we live for today, doing the work He assigns us, we will live our dreams and see His come true.

- God is always working behind the scenes, fulfilling His plan, and growing His kingdom.
- We rejoice knowing He is working all things out for our good, the good of others, and His glory.

Dream Work:

- What price are you paying to live your dream?
- Make a list of your current commitments. Are there any you need to eliminate to have time and energy for your dream?
- How is God using you to grow His kingdom?
- List the talents and gifts God has given you. How is He calling you to use these to build the body of Christ?
- What worries about your dream do you need to surrender to God?
- Prayerfully write a dream plan that will help you prepare to work on your dream as you move forward on your dream path.
- How can you fix your eyes on the eternal as you work your dream?

Chapter 11
Dreams Fulfilled

We have finally come to the first fulfillment of Joseph's dream. He dreamed so many years ago about sheaves of wheat and the stars bowing down to him (Genesis 37:7-9). Now over twenty years later, had he forgotten his original dreams? Even if he had dismissed them and resigned himself to make the most of his new life, we can be sure that when he saw his brothers bowing before him memories of his God-given dream reappeared.

Circumstances of life may obscure our dreams. Even happy, fruitful times may cause our minds to stray from our dreams. But God never forgets. He is a promise maker and a promise keeper. He continues to act behind the scenes and will remind us of our God-given dreams when we need a refresher. The fulfillment of our dreams may surprise us as much as they did Joseph. His dream was headed straight toward him from his homeland.

Joseph's brothers traveled to the land of Egypt and bowed before the person in charge of selling grain, not knowing it was Joseph. Joseph recognized them, remembered his dream, but pretended to be a stranger. He spoke harshly to them and accused them of being spies who came to see where the land of Egypt was unprotected. The brothers insisted they were from the land of Canaan who had come to buy food. When Joseph continued to insist, they were spies, they added there were originally twelve brothers, but one brother remained with their father, and the other one was dead (Genesis 42:6-13).

Can you imagine how Joseph felt standing before the ones who had thrown him in a pit to die, then rescued him, and sold him into slavery? He may have wondered if time had corrected their disposition. So, Joseph came up with a test to see if they had changed.

Joseph instructed them to choose one brother to go get their younger brother and bring him back to Egypt. Joseph would keep the other nine imprisoned until their youngest brother came. Then he held all of them in prison. After three days, Joseph changed the plan because he feared God. He decided he would hold one brother and allowed the others to return home with grain for their families. When they brought their youngest brother to Egypt, he would believe their story, release the brothers from prison, and sell them more grain. The brothers agreed to the condition, but among themselves, they discussed whether they were being punished for what they had done to Joseph years earlier. When Joseph heard this, he wept (Genesis 42:20-24).

The brothers were getting a small taste of what Joseph suffered. He experienced slavery and prison for thirteen years. Joseph held them in prison for three days. Perhaps they often thought of and discussed among themselves the wrong they did to Joseph. Now, faced with the thought of having to take Benjamin, the only living son of Rachel, away from his father, they decided they were finally facing the punishment they deserved.

There will be times along our dream paths when God tests us. If we have made mistakes and confessed them, He has forgiven us. But

He may send tests to see if we have learned from them. Our dream journeys include building the character to live our dreams. God was also testing Joseph as Joseph tested the brothers. Had Joseph forgiven them? Would he use this opportunity to retaliate against them for selling him into slavery?

Joseph hoped his brothers had changed, but he needed to continue with the test to see if it were true. He bound Simeon but ordered his servants to release the other nine and sell them grain. He also ordered the steward to put each of the men's money in his sack. The brothers loaded their donkeys and headed home. When they stopped for the night and opened their sacks to feed their donkeys, each man found the money. They trembled, thinking God was repaying them for the harm they did to Joseph when he was young, but they continued home, and told Jacob what happened. Jacob was distraught and declared, "You have deprived me of my children. Joseph is no more, and Simeon is no more, and now you want to take Benjamin. Everything is against me!" (Genesis 42:24-36).

Sometimes when we study the story of Joseph and all he endured, we fail to think about poor Jacob. He endured much suffering in losing his beloved wife, Rachel, during childbirth. He had lost his favored son, Joseph, by death to a wild beast (at least, he thought he had). After many years of learning to live with these losses, now famine struck and a trip to get food led to the loss of another son, Simeon, and threatened to take Benjamin from him.

Jacob had also experienced the loss of his dream. God gave Jacob a dream of angels ascending and descending on a stairway to and from heaven. Above it, the Lord appeared to him and reconfirmed the promise He gave to his grandfather Abraham to bless him with many descendants and give them the land of Canaan (Genesis 28:10-14). Whether Jacob believed God would fulfill this promise through his remaining ten sons, he still felt the loss of the two he now mourned. God might still fulfill his dream, but not how Jacob wished. Or at least it didn't appear God would.

When we face the death of our dreams or wonder how God could do what we think He has promised, we can hold on to what He has spoken through His Word. To Jacob, He promised, "I am with you and will watch over you wherever you go, and I will bring you back to this land. I will not leave you until I have done what I have promised you" (Genesis 28:15). The same is true for us. God will fulfill every promise in His Word, and He will fulfill the plans He has for us. We need not figure out how He will. We can just trust He will.

Jacob resigned himself to protecting the part of the dream he had left. He declared his youngest son would not go to Egypt. He felt if he lost Benjamin, he would die from sorrow (Genesis 42:38).

When we feel like Jacob, that everything is against us and part of our dreams are dead, we can remind ourselves God's plan has not changed. Romans 8:28 assures us "that in all things God works for the good of those who love him, who have been called according to his purpose." God works all things for good—the good, the bad, the planned, the unplanned, what we do, and what others do to us. All things. He works all things for our good because we have been called according to His purpose. His plan for us remains intact. He will work it to its fulfillment just as He was doing in the life of Jacob and his whole family.

We can choose to trust Him and keep living the plan by being faithful and obedient. When we refuse to follow the plan as God lays it out, He will do whatever it takes to get us back on the path to our dreams. He did this with Jacob, who declared Benjamin would not go down to Egypt.

Jacob might have thought they could ride out the famine. He did not know what Joseph and the Egyptians knew - the famine would last seven years. But God knew and was determined to move Jacob and his family to Egypt. God told Abraham, Jacob's grandfather, their family would serve as slaves in a foreign land for four hundred years and then He would bring them out with great wealth (Genesis 15:13-14). This was the plan God was fulfilling. God orchestrated the famine to move Jacob and his family to Egypt. Neither Jacob, the brothers, nor anyone else could stop God from fulfilling His promise.

No one can stop God's purpose in our lives. Three verses in Philippians challenge us to believe God and trust Him to work in and through us. Philippians 1:6– "Being confident of this, that he who began a good work in you will carry it on to completion until the day of Christ Jesus." Philippians 2:13– "For it is God who works in you to will and to act in order to fulfill his good purpose." And Philippians 4:13– "I can do all this through him who gives me strength."

When we choose to believe these verses, we can have confidence God will complete the work He has for us. It's God who inspires us to dream for Him and works through us to fulfill those dreams. His Holy Spirit empowers us to do everything required to fulfill our God-given dreams. He will do whatever is necessary to continue to push us down the path to the dream.

God allowed the famine to continue until Jacob, and his family ate all the grain. Jacob instructed his sons to go back to Egypt to buy more food. Judah reminded him there would be no benefit of going without Benjamin, for the man in charge had told them they would not see him again unless they brought their youngest brother and proved they were not spies. But Judah assured Jacob he would keep Benjamin safe, and if anything happened to him, Jacob could hold him personally responsible (Genesis 43:1-10).

It's interesting to me Judah was the one who spoke up saying he will protect Benjamin. If we remember what happened to Joseph, it was Reuben who planned to rescue Joseph from the pit and return him to his father. Judah was the one who came up with the plan to sell their brother to the Ishmaelites (Genesis 37:26-27). Perhaps Judah learned his lesson. Maybe he felt the guilt more fully than the other brothers, being the oldest and most directly responsible for Joseph's fate.

Finally, Jacob agreed, saying, "If it must be." Then he gave them instructions to take balm, honey, spices, myrrh, pistachios, and almonds as a gift to the man in charge in Egypt. In addition, they were to take double the amount of silver they paid for the first grain; to return the silver they found in their sacks and then buy more grain. Jacob hoped the silver in the sacks was a mistake and sent them away praying, "And may God Almighty grant you mercy before the man so that he will let your other brother and Benjamin come back with you. As for me, if I am bereaved, I am bereaved" (Genesis 43:11-14).

Although it sounds fatalistic, sometimes we must move forward with our lives saying, "If it must be." When circumstances dictate what we do, we can trust even though we have no control, God does.

Nothing surprises God. Everything that happens to us has already passed through the hands of our loving Father. When our situation seems bleak and we wonder why God would allow what is happening, we can say, "If it must be" and continue to serve God to the best of our ability.

We should also pray for God to grant us and others mercy. God may or may not choose to change our situations. Sometimes He responds to our prayers by giving us what we request.

God gave Hezekiah what he asked for. When Hezekiah became gravely ill, God sent a prophet to tell him he would die. Hezekiah wept bitterly and cried to God asking Him to spare his life. God sent the prophet back to Hezekiah to let him know God granted his request, healed him, and allowed him to live fifteen more years (2 Kings 20:1-6).

When my mom was diagnosed with cancer in 2004, she was given a five-year prognosis. Others advised me to pray for complete healing. While I knew God was a miracle-working God, I also knew sometimes He uses suffering in the lives of His children. I asked God was it my mom's time to die or if He planned to heal her. Although I did not receive peace a full healing would come, I felt led to pray as Hezekiah had. I asked God to give her fifteen more years. He honored my prayer. Although mom's cancer battle included radiation, many chemotherapy treatments, and five surgeries, God extended her life. She passed in 2022, over fifteen years after I prayed. He granted her the fifteen years I asked for and more.

God may not always grant us what we ask, but He will always give us mercy. "Let us then approach God's throne of grace with confidence, so that we may receive mercy and find grace to help us in our time of need" (Hebrews 4:16). We can boldly approach our Father in prayer knowing He has promised we will receive mercy and grace to help us in our time of need.

The brothers headed to Egypt for the second time, hoping the man in charge would show them mercy and give them what they needed. They presented themselves and Benjamin to him, and he invited them to his home for a meal. The brothers were frightened, thinking Joseph was looking for retribution because of the money they found in their sacks the first trip. They proclaim, "He wants to attack us and overpower us and seize us as slaves and take our donkeys" (Genesis 43:15-18).

Isn't it odd the brothers not only feared Joseph attacking, overpowering them, and forcing them into slavery, but also taking their donkeys? This might serve as a reminder to us not to worry about small things. Worrying about the unnecessary will keep us from doing the most important. The brothers should have been worrying about themselves and the life of their brother Simeon, who was still being held by Joseph, and Benjamin, whom Jacob was so concerned about.

The same temptation may overcome us. When our circumstances turn unexpectedly, Satan would love to have us worrying about our donkeys. The donkeys represent earthly treasures, like our possessions, hobbies, or even our reputations. We are to trust God with these and focus on advancing His kingdom through obedience. Matthew 6:19-32 warns us not to store up earthly treasures and not to worry about our physical lives and the things involved with them, like food and clothing. We can trust our Heavenly Father to provide everything we need. He promises, "Seek first his kingdom and his righteousness, and all these things will be given to you as well. Therefore do not worry about tomorrow, for tomorrow will worry about itself. Each day has enough trouble of its own" (Matthew 6:33-34).

As I've lived my dreams, I've often worried about what others think of me. I worry about what I'm wearing or how I look. I often fret over my Southern accent and wonder if I sound too country. Other times, I replay previous lessons in my head, dissecting and criticizing them. In doing this, I waste time I could use to prepare the next lesson. Sometimes, I worry about finances and am tempted to give up my dream of ministering full time instead of trusting God to provide what I need. All these are 'donkeys' distracting me from focusing on doing the work God has assigned.

When the brothers arrived at Joseph's house, they spoke to the steward about the money they found in their sacks on the first trip. They told him they brought the money back along with additional money to buy more grain. The steward assured them not to be afraid. He had their money. He asserted God had given them the treasure they found in their sacks. The steward then brought out Simeon, provided water to wash their feet and fodder for their donkeys (Genesis 43:19-24).

I can't help but chuckle as the steward cared for the donkeys they worried about. Isn't this what God promised in Matthew 6? We don't have to worry about our earthly needs. God will take care of us as we are busy doing His business.

Years ago, my husband stepped out of his work truck, twisted his ankle, and heard a pop. After painfully driving home, he had an x-ray and confirmed it was broken. He received a cast and instructions he could not work until it healed. The next twelve weeks were a trying time financially, but God proved Himself faithful. He provided all we needed, and He taught us to trust Him more fully.

The brothers were learning to trust God. They presented the gift they brought and bowed down to the ground before Joseph. Joseph asked about their father. They said he was well and bowed down again, prostrating themselves before him. When Joseph saw Benjamin, his brother from his own mother, he was deeply moved and hurried out to his private room to weep (Genesis 43:25-30).

We have just seen the second fulfillment of Joseph's dream. Twice now, the brothers have bowed before Joseph, just as he dreamed they would. The brothers didn't know it was Joseph, their long-lost brother, standing before them, but Joseph did. Can you even imagine what Joseph was feeling? He was getting to see the brothers he thought he had lost forever, and he was seeing God fulfill his dream right before his eyes.

It had been over twenty years, but God was faithful. He is a promise keeper who does what He says He will do. Since God has given us our dreams, we can trust Him to fulfill them just as He did in Joseph's life. Even if we have not discovered our God-given dreams, we can trust He is working them through us. He will reveal and fulfill them as we serve Him faithfully.

First Thessalonians 5:24 assures us, "The one who calls you is faithful, and he will do it." We don't make our dreams come true. God does—He is the Dream-giver and the Dream-fulfiller. We can trust Him and be "confident of this, that he who began a good work in you will carry it on to completion until the day of Christ Jesus" (Philippians 1:6).

Dream Notes:

- God is the Dream-giver, Dream-leader, and Dream-fulfiller.
- We can trust Him to reveal and fulfill our dreams as we serve Him faithfully.
- Even when our dreams seem dead, we can know God will fulfill every promise in His Word, and He will empower us to fulfill the plans He has for us.
- God will remind us of our God-given dreams and may surprise us by how He fulfills them.
- Our dream journeys include tests that build character to live our dreams.
- God works all things for our good because we have been called according to His purpose.
- We can choose to trust Him and keep living the plan by being faithful and obedient.
- When circumstances dictate what we do, we can remember God is still in control, nothing surprises Him, and everything happening has already passed through His hands.
- If we refuse to follow God's plan, He will do whatever it takes to draw us back onto our dream paths.

- When our circumstances turn unexpectedly, we are to trust God, stop worrying about the less important things, and focus on advancing His kingdom through obedience.

Dream Work:

- What tests have you experienced on your dream path?
- What did God teach you through them?
- When have you felt like everything was against you?
- How did you work through the doubt and keep moving forward with your dream?
- Consider memorizing Philippians 1:6, 2:13, and 4:13. (This power-trio will give you confidence to trust God to complete your dream.)
- How are you fully trusting God to provide all you need to make your God-given dream come true?

Chapter 12
Don't Miss Your Dream

We left Joseph's brothers bowing before him, fulfilling his dream. One might wonder–Did the brothers have dreams of their own? I would like to suggest they did. Just as God created Joseph and placed him in Jacob's family exactly as He designed, so He did with each brother. The brothers may not have been aware of their dreams, but God was fulfilling them just as He had planned.

God gives each of us a dream. Even if we don't have a clear sense of the dreams God has planned for us, we can serve Him, trusting He is working His plan. We may make mistakes along our dream paths, yet nothing will cause us to lose our dreams. He will continue working in each of our lives until He has fulfilled the dreams He has for us just as He did with Joseph and his brothers.

The brothers didn't realize Joseph's dream involved them. They were to be the future heads of the twelve tribes of Israel, but jealousy of Joseph's dream prevented them from considering the dream might have been for their benefit. All they could think was Joseph should never rule over them. They missed that by trying to stop Joseph's dream they were really messing with the working out of their own. Yet even their mistreatment of Joseph did not negate the plan God had for them. He was working all things through them to advance His ultimate plan for the nation of Israel and the world.

We really don't know what would have happened if the brothers had not sold Joseph into slavery, but his family, the Israelites, would have faced slavery in a foreign land for four hundred years by some means because God had predicted they would (Genesis 15:13). It was part of God's dream for the world that was being fulfilled through the nation of Israel.

God will fulfill His plans for all His people. We may make wrong choices delaying or changing the details of how our dreams are fulfilled, but we can't stop God from doing what He is going to do. If we believe this, do our actions along the way matter? Of course they do.

God is teaching us and drawing us closer to Himself. How we walk our dream paths affects our relationship with Him and might even determine how quickly we arrive at the place of full blessing and service. Disobedience, sin, or selfishness may delay our dreams but will not negate them. We should also keep in mind the choices we make have consequences.

God called Jonah to go preach to Ninevah. Jonah ran in the opposite direction and landed in the belly of a great fish. After three days of suffering, he repented, was spit out by the fish, and headed in the right direction. In doing so, he was obeying and fulfilling God's dream for him. Although the Bible doesn't directly say it, he must have borne the marks of disobedience. As he marched through Nineveh declaring the judgment of God would come if they didn't repent, his own skin testified to the cost of running from God's plan (Jonah 1:1-17 and 2:1,10).

We suffer when we refuse to move forward with God's plan, but God remains resolved to push the plan forward as He did with Joseph and his brothers. He has a way of bringing all things together for good.

I've been slow and sometimes resistant to walk forward in my dream of writing for God. One time, at a writer's conference, I fell on my bed and exclaimed, "I don't want to do this. It's too hard." God gently responded, "What makes you think you have a choice?" Although I could have refused to get up, dry my face, and move forward with His dream for me, I would have been miserable if I had. I knew He called me to speak and write for Him, and I could only experience genuine joy if I did my best to be obedient.

Since then, I've faced other steps I hesitated to take, but each time God prodded me forward. I've already shared how He is opening many doors for me to teach for Him. He has given me the opportunity to write this book, and I am trying to be obedient. I may make mistakes along my path, but I can trust He is guiding me and providing the strength I need to walk in His way. We can trust God to equip us and provide everything we need to bring us to our dreams.

God reunited Joseph with his brothers just as He planned, but God wasn't finished maturing the brothers. He would use Benjamin to see if they learned from the evil they had committed against Joseph. Joseph invited the brothers to his home for a meal and instructed his servants to sit them in birth order. The servant gave Benjamin five times as much food as he gave the other brothers. They all feasted and drank freely, but Joseph sat at a separate table still pretending to be an Egyptian (Genesis 43:31-34).

Joseph remembered one reason the brothers hated him was because of the special favoritism Jacob showed him. He showed Benjamin special treatment to see if they would also hate Benjamin for it. He continued with the plan by ordering his steward to fill their sacks with grain, put their money in the top as before, and to place his silver cup in Benjamin's sack. The next day, he sent them on their way (Genesis 44:1-3).

Before the brothers went very far, Joseph sent his steward after them, instructing him to apprehend Benjamin for stealing the cup. When the steward caught up with them, he accused them of repaying good with evil by stealing Joseph's cup. The brothers denied the allegations and attested to their honesty by stating how they brought back the silver they had found inside the mouths of their sacks the last time. They challenged the accusation by asking why they would steal silver or gold this time. Then they made a fatal pledge: "If any of your servants is found to have it, he will die; and the rest of us will become my lord's slaves" (Genesis 44:4-9).

The brothers' response showed great trust of each other. They could not imagine any of them stole the cup. However, their promise to be slaves was rash and showed little care for their own lives or for the feelings of their father Jacob, not thinking of how he would mourn if none of them returned. Perhaps they forgot the promise God had given to their great-grandfather, Abraham, saying He would make them a great nation (Genesis 12:2), or they failed to see their role in fulfilling that dream. They were not living purposefully for the dream. They were simply existing. However, God continued to work out all details sovereignly to advance His promise and His dream.

God has called us all to fulfill His dream. We each have our part. We live the dream by obediently taking each step He directs. My uncle would probably say he doesn't have a dream. He just lives his life helping others in need. I would say this is his dream. He has turned down the position of deacon at his church many times, but he lives like one. As a deacon is a servant, my uncle is a deacon by work but not by title. He visits the sick and homebound, gives vegetables from his garden to those in need, and regularly gives money to widows. He is living his God-given dream of spreading the love of Jesus to the less fortunate.

We live out our God-given dreams as we serve God by serving others. As we do, we should carefully consider what we commit to. Once our children's ministry leader asked me to work in children's church, which involved serving on Sunday mornings eight to twelve times a year. I was already serving in other areas, but desiring to do whatever was asked of me, I headed to the leader to agree to the position. Walking down the hallway, twenty feet from the commitment, God corrected me. He said to me, "I did not tell you to do this." I proceeded to the person and politely declined the job. I felt very uncomfortable doing so but was later relieved that I didn't commit to a job God did not call me to.

Since then, I've learned to pray and wait for God to give clear instructions. I've also learned not to feel bad about saying no. Less time and energy will be available for the jobs God assigns if I take a position He does not appoint. I might also hinder the person He is calling to the position from accepting it.

Because we do not know what God is working behind the scenes, we need to be careful to follow His leading in every area. We also don't know how Satan is trying to trick us or attempting to steal our dreams. Although he cannot, we don't want to suffer the consequences that may come with a wrong turn. It's best if we head straight toward our dreams, listen carefully to our Dream coach, and stay firmly on the dream paths until we reach them.

The brothers obligated themselves to be slaves and stated the one with the stolen cup would die, but the steward replied he would only take the guilty party as a slave. The rest would be free. All the brothers lowered their sacks and opened them for inspection. The steward began his search with the oldest and proceeded to the youngest. One by one he cleared the bags until he came to Benjamin. To the brother's astonishment, the cup was found in Benjamin's sack. The brothers tore their clothes in distress and rushed back to the city to beg for Benjamin's release (Genesis 44:10-13).

The brothers passed the first portion of the test. They did not abandon Benjamin even though he appeared guilty. The brothers entered Joseph's house and threw themselves to the ground before him. Joseph questioned them, and Judah spoke for the group, asking what they could do to prove their innocence. He pledged they all would be Joseph's slaves. Joseph refused by saying, "Far be it from me to do such a thing! Only the man who was found to have the cup will become my slave. The rest of you, go back to your father in peace" (Genesis 44:14-17).

At this point, the brothers have passed three tests. They returned with Benjamin to free Simeon. Benjamin receiving more food from the servants did not phase them. They pled for Benjamin's release when the cup was found in his sack. Would they pass the fourth? Faced with the option of abandoning Benjamin, would they opt to save their own lives, return home without him, and tell Jacob they had done all they could do to free him?

Judah again speaks to Joseph, reminding him how Joseph asked if they had a father or a brother. He recounted how they answered honestly by telling him, "We have an aged father, and there is a young son born to him in his old age. His brother is dead, and he is the only one of his mother's sons left, and his father loves him." Judah told him how Jacob refused to let Benjamin go to Egypt for fear of losing him like he lost his brother. Jacob urged them to go buy more food, but the brothers insisted they could not go without Benjamin. Seeing they might all starve, Jacob relented and let him go. Judah told how Jacob said if anything happened to Benjamin, he would die of misery. Judah begged Joseph to keep him instead of Benjamin to spare his father from dying of grief (Genesis 44:18-33).

The brothers seem to have learned their lesson. Still thinking Joseph was dead, they refused to cause their father the same grief twice. They begged Joseph to let Benjamin return to Jacob. They have learned to stick together and look out for each other. Although Benjamin had taken Joseph's place as the favored son, the brothers were no longer jealous, nor did they hate Benjamin as they did Joseph. Watching Jacob mourn Joseph may have caused them to care more for their father's feelings than their own. They may have learned not to compare themselves to others. Having their own families, they have matured and have more to worry about than whose dream was the best.

Judah's actions show he has experienced a radical transformation. He had been the brother who suggested they sell Joseph into slavery. Having promised his father, he would take care of Benjamin, he was now willing to take Benjamin's place to gain his freedom. This foreshadows Jesus' coming to take our place by dying on the cross, so we can live for God. Interestingly, Jesus came from the line of Judah (Matthew 1:1-16). All the events in the life of Joseph's family work to progress God's dream of delivering all people from sin and bring them to Himself. These events culminated in the substitutionary death of His Son on the cross. Through accepting Him as Savior, we gain eternal life and begin living our God-given dreams which serve to bring others to Him.

As we mature, we learn all have dreams, and we shouldn't compare them to the dreams of others. God has His plans for each of us. My dream does not negate your dream, nor does yours negate mine. Actually, each of us living our dreams helps others live theirs. God calls us to be a body of believers that works together to accomplish His dream. If we compete with others, we hinder His work. Me living my dream helps you live yours, and vice versa. We can be encouraged when we see others using their gifts and talents for God.

Part of my husband's dream has always been to help me live mine. He worked many hours to provide financially so I could stay home to raise and homeschool our children. He often does extra housework when I need to write lessons and meet deadlines, even though he works a full-time job. And he never complains if the house is messy or we have takeout.

We can guard against comparing and focus on what is important, others. The first time the brothers found their money in their sacks, they were worried about their donkeys. This time, facing the loss of their brother and knowing the grief it would cause their father, there was no mention of the donkeys. They have learned to focus on what matters most.

As we serve God and live our dreams, we are wise to focus on others. Living our dreams is about helping others and glorifying God. It isn't a competition but a collaboration. We are to be working together for the same goal, advancing the kingdom of God. We can't do that if we are comparing or competing.

Jesus said, "If a house is divided against itself, that house cannot stand" (Mark 3:25). We are all members of the house of God who are to be building each other up and working together to fulfill God's dream. We do this by focusing on the portion of the dream God gives us, while also helping others fulfill their dreams.

God gave the brothers a second chance. The test Joseph presented forced them to confront their past actions toward him and gave them the opportunity to reveal their new character. It revealed they were now committed to each other.

Our God is the God of second chances, and third, fourth, fifth, and more. He is always ready to forgive us for our mistakes and set us back on our dream paths. He will ensure we realize the dreams He has for us.

Dream Notes:

- God gives us dreams that match His plan, and He will ensure the realization of those dreams if we cooperate with Him.

- Even if we don't have a clear sense of the dreams God has planned for us, we can serve Him, trusting He is working His plan.

- We may make wrong choices, delaying or changing the details of how our dreams are fulfilled, but we can't stop God from doing what He is going to do.

- The choices we make along our dream paths have consequences.

- How we walk the dream paths affects our relationship with Him and might even determine how quickly we arrive at the place of full blessing and service.

- Disobedience, sin, or selfishness may delay our dreams, but God is ready to forgive and set us back on our dream paths.

- We walk forward on the path to fulfilling our God-given dreams by:
  - praying and waiting for God to give clear instructions.
  - listening to Him and obediently taking every step, He directs.
  - following His lead by carefully considering what we commit to.
  - staying firmly on the dream paths until we reach the dream.

- Living the dream with other believers is a collaboration, not a competition.

- We are to work together in advancing the kingdom of God through helping others and glorifying God.

Dream Work:

- What mistakes have you made on your dream path?
- If you have not, confess them now and ask God to help you move forward.
- When have you refused to take a step God directed?
- What consequences did you face for your disobedience?
- How did God set you back on the path to your dream?
- What step is God currently calling you to make?
- Write a prayer of commitment to obey in your dream journal.
- Ask for wisdom and strength to continue down the path until you reach your God-given dream.

Chapter 13
Dreams Come True

We have seen the actual fulfilment of Joseph's dreams through his brothers bowing before him twice. But Joseph's dream was not over. He was now living exalted in the land of Egypt, but he was still separated from his family. His dream encompassed so much more than he could have surmised from the original dreams God gave him at seventeen. Joseph's dream was a smaller part of God's big dream to spread knowledge of Himself to the entire world. God used the fulfillment of Joseph's God-given dream to advance His plan. He would move Jacob's family to Egypt just as He declared previously to their ancestors.

Our God-given dreams, no matter how big or small, are also part of God fulfilling His ultimate plan of bringing people to Himself through salvation. As we live our dreams, our focus should be on bringing others to God.

> All this is from God, who reconciled us to himself through Christ and gave us the ministry of reconciliation: that God was reconciling the world to himself in Christ, not counting people's sins against them. And he has committed to us the message of reconciliation. We are therefore Christ's ambassadors, as though God were making his appeal through us. We implore you on Christ's behalf: Be reconciled to God. (2 Corinthians 5:18-20)

Reconciliation is a bringing back together. God created us for relationship and fellowship. Sin separated us from Him, but Jesus paid the price to reconnect us to God. God restores fellowship with believers through Jesus and calls us to help others come back to Him. We serve as God's ambassadors by appealing to those around us to accept the gift of salvation offered through Jesus and be reconnected to God.

We will see how God also uses Joseph as a minister of reconciliation. His brothers separated themselves from him by selling him into slavery. They took him away from Jacob and hid their treachery from their father. This separated them relationally from their father, as all lies separate us from the one to whom we lie. But God reconnected their family and demonstrated the forgiveness He offers all people through Joseph's forgiveness of them.

When Joseph saw his brothers would not abandon Benjamin, he began to weep. He ordered his attendants to leave him alone with them. In private, he revealed himself to his brothers, saying, "I am Joseph! Is my father still living?" The brothers stood speechless with fear. Joseph continued, "'Come close to me.' When they had done so, he said, 'I am your brother Joseph, the one you sold into Egypt!'" (Genesis 45:1-4). Joseph could have hated his brothers for all they took from him, but he loved and forgave them despite the years of separation and heartache.

A willingness to exercise love and forgiveness shows we are children of God. Jesus proclaimed, "A new command I give you: Love one another. As I have loved you, so you must love one another. By this everyone will know that you are my disciples, if you love one another" (John 13:34-35). Jesus commands us to love each other with the same type of love He has for us. He displayed His love for us on Calvary, where He willingly hung on the cross, suffering the punishment you and I deserve. He allowed the sins of every person ever created to be placed on Him and then experienced the wrath of God for those sins. Through this, He gave us the opportunity to be born again and become reconciled to God, giving us new life with new dreams that line up with His.

As we live our dreams, we are to reflect God and His love to the world. God's love was selfless and sacrificial. In the same manner which He died for us, we display His love by willingly pouring out our lives for those around us. Living our dreams is about ministering to others through loving them as God does. Just as Joseph loved his brothers, we are to love all people around us.

God convicted me early in my ministry to love others. I grew up loving and studying His word, but I didn't always find it as easy to love people. To be able to help them know God through His word, I needed to relate to them as He did, in love. I began to pray that God would help me love others, and He did. He poured His love through me to the ones I serve.

The brothers did not know how Joseph would react to them. Remembering what they did to Joseph, they stood terrified before him. Seeing their fear, Joseph comforted them, saying, "Do not be distressed and do not be angry with yourselves for selling me here, because it was to save lives that God sent me ahead of you." He explained the famine which had already lasted for two years would continue for five more. He encouraged them by saying God sent him to Egypt to preserve a remnant and to save their lives with a great deliverance. He assured them again their selling him as a slave was part of God's plan, and he explained he was master over Pharaoh's household and was ruler over all of Egypt (Genesis 45:5-8).

Joseph displayed the love called for in Ephesians 4:2 which says, "Be completely humble and gentle; be patient, bearing with one another in love." Joseph expressed his humility by saying God was the one who sent him to Egypt. He was gentle and patient as he reassured them not to be afraid or angry with themselves for selling him. Joseph learned through his trials to bear the burdens God placed upon him, and now he will continue by bearing his brother's burdens because he loved them.

Joseph was in a position of power, which could have been used to retaliate against his brothers, but he forgave. In Second Corinthians 13:11, God calls us to have this same attitude. "Finally, brothers and sisters, rejoice! Strive for full restoration, encourage one another, be of one mind, live in peace. And the God of love and peace will be with you." Despite others having mistreated us in the past, we are to strive to restore the relationship. We can exercise mutual respect for others, seek unity with them, and pursue peace, especially among other believers.

Ministry often gives us opportunities to practice forgiveness. In the past, I have been accused of saying things I did not say and other things I've said have been taken out of context. In each of these situations, I chose to forgive the people involved. Another time, when I heard false rumors circulating about me, I had to seek out the person spreading them and try to work things out. When she confessed and asked for forgiveness, I chose to forgive her and restore the friendship.

Forgiveness is important for faithful service. God calls us to "Bear with each other and forgive one another if any of you has a grievance against someone. Forgive as the Lord forgave you" (Colossians 3:13). Forgiving as God did is hard, but with His help we can do it.

Joseph could forgive his brothers because he understood God's sovereignty. Three times Joseph declared God sent him. He knew God controlled all things. God allowed him to be sold as a slave and thrown into prison and had now exalted him as a leader. He assured his brothers God sent him to Egypt to save them and many others.

As we live our dreams, we can remember God controls all things. God may allow others to trouble us to prepare us to serve Him. God determines any exaltation we receive. All exaltation—in our church, community, work, or family—is for the good of those around us. We can use our positions to glorify God through serving others. We are not to look out for our own interest but seek to bless the ones to whom we are called to minister. James 4:10 instructs, "Humble yourselves before the Lord, and he will lift you up."

Early in my call to ministry, God convicted me to pray for humility. I asked Him not to place me in any position if I would not be humble. As I began to teach and received compliments, I continued to pray for humbleness. I often tell God I know I can't do it without His help. He is the one who gifted me to teach, and I rely on Him to help me do it.

Joseph humbly used his position to bless others. He offered grace to his brothers through forgiveness, generosity, and care. Joseph instructed his brothers to hurry back to their father and tell him, "This is what your son Joseph says: God has made me lord of all Egypt. Come down to me; don't delay." He invited Jacob to bring his whole family—his children and grandchildren, his flocks and herds, and all he owned and come live in Goshen so they could be near Joseph. He promised to provide for them during the next five years of famine and warned if they did not come, they would become destitute (Genesis 45:9-11).

He encouraged them again, saying, "You can see for yourselves, and so can my brother Benjamin, that it is really I who am speaking to you. Tell my father about all the honor accorded me in Egypt and about everything you have seen. And bring my father down here quickly." Then Joseph embraced Benjamin and his other brothers. He wept over them and kissed them (Genesis 45:12-15).

Joseph seeing, hugging, and kissing his brothers is a beautiful picture of restoration. He called for his father and the rest of his family to come. Can you imagine the joy he would experience when he saw his father again after so many years? Or the excitement of meeting his sisters-in-law and his nieces and nephews?

God loves restoration. Jesus stated, "I tell you that in the same way there will be more rejoicing in heaven over one sinner who repents than over ninety-nine righteous persons who do not need to repent" (Luke 15:7). In Luke 15, Jesus told three parables—one about a lost sheep, another about a lost coin, and the last about a lost son. In each of the parables, the person who lost the item searched diligently for it. The shepherd left ninety-nine sheep to look for his lost sheep. The woman swept her entire house to find her lost coin. Both the shepherd and the woman called their friends together to rejoice when they found what had been lost (Luke 15:6 and 9). The father in the last parable watched every day to see his wayward son return. When he did, the father ran to him, embraced him, and called the servants to bring a robe and ring for him. (Luke 15:22). The father rejoiced, "For this son of mine was dead and is alive again; he was lost and is found" (Luke 15:24).

These are all pictures of how our Heavenly Father rejoices over each lost sinner who comes to Him through salvation. We often think of the joy of reuniting with our loved ones in heaven. While this will be wonderful, it fails compared to being reunited fully with God our Father. Joseph rejoiced to see his brothers, but oh how Jacob would rejoice when he learned Joseph was alive and was calling him to come live in Egypt with him.

Pharaoh heard Joseph's brothers had come and sent word to Joseph to send for his father and the rest of the family. He pledged to give them the best land in Egypt and sent carts for them to bring the children back to Egypt. Pharaoh declared the family didn't need to bring their personal belongings because he would give them the best of Egypt (Genesis 45:16-20). Through this, God continued to bless through Joseph.

Joseph sent his brothers home to Canaan with carts loaded with provisions for their journey. To each brother, he gave new clothing, but to Benjamin he gave three hundred shekels of silver and five sets of clothes. To his father, he sent twenty donkeys loaded with the best things of Egypt, which included grain and bread and other provisions for the family's journey. As the brothers left, Joseph instructed them, "Don't quarrel on the way!" (Genesis 45:21-24).

Joseph instructing them not to quarrel is interesting. Although the brothers showed maturity, Joseph may have worried they would blame each other for the initial crime against him. Or he might have thought the stress of moving their families and all they owned to Egypt would resurface their old habit of quarreling.

Change, good or bad, can bring out the worst in our character. Stress can make us short-tempered with the ones we serve. Practicing self-care, such as eating healthy, exercising regularly, and getting proper rest, will provide energy and stamina to continue serving in our dreams. The challenges and busyness of ministry can lead to stress. Staying aware of our stress levels and taking breaks when we need them can also help guard against impatience and other unwanted behavior.

Reminding ourselves that each challenge is an opportunity to serve our Master can help us guard against impatience. God tells us how to clothe ourselves for ministry in Colossians 3:12-13. It says, "Therefore, as God's chosen people, holy and dearly loved, clothe yourselves with compassion, kindness, humility, gentleness and patience. Bear with each other and forgive one another if any of you has a grievance against someone. Forgive as the Lord forgave you." While we can't develop these traits on our own, we can trust God to pour them in and through us as we submit to Him. Through Him, we can exercise patience and love others. He helps us bear with and forgive others because the ones we are called to serve aren't always easy to love.

Joseph's brothers arrived home and told Jacob, "Joseph is still alive! In fact, he is ruler of all Egypt." Stunned, Jacob did not believe them until he saw the carts and all the provisions Joseph sent. When Jacob believed their report, his spirit revived. Finally, Jacob exclaimed, "I'm convinced! My son Joseph is still alive. I will go and see him before I die" (Genesis 45:25-28).

Oh, what joy must have filled Jacob's heart. Not only did he received Benjamin, whom he feared would be lost, and Simeon, who had been held in Egypt, but also Joseph, whom he considered long dead. His dream of God creating a nation through all twelve of his sons was revived (Genesis 35:11). He would now go to Egypt, see his long-lost son Joseph, and have his whole family together again. And God would provide all he and his family needed through the fulfillment of Joseph's dream.

God's dream is to bring all men to Himself. First Timothy 2:4 declares, "[God] wants all people to be saved and to come to a knowledge of the truth." He sent His Son, Jesus, so men and women could have the opportunity to return to Him. "For God so loved the world that he gave his one and only Son, that whoever believes in him shall not perish but have eternal life. For God did not send his Son into the world to condemn the world, but to save the world through him" (John 3:16-17).

We get to share in God's dream as we tell others about Jesus and show them how they can be reconciled to Him. He uses our God-given dreams to help others know and love Him. Let us be faithful to God and to those He appoints us to tell.

Dream Notes:
- Our dreams encompass much more than we can imagine.
- Our God-given dreams, big and small, work together to fulfill God's ultimate plan of bringing people to Himself through salvation.
- We get to share in His dream as we tell others about Jesus.
- God, having created us for relationship and fellowship, calls us to help others come back to Him.
- As we live our dreams, we minister to others by exercising the love and forgiveness that God has shown us.
- Looking at every challenge as an opportunity to serve our Master can help us exercise patience and love others like He does.
- God calls us to have compassion, kindness, humility, gentleness, and patience as we serve.
- Living our dreams may involve challenges and busyness leading to stress.
- Staying aware of our stress levels and practicing self-care can keep us energized for ministry.
- We can be patient and persistent as we spread the message of the goodness and grace of God.

Dream Work:

- In what ways has the fulfillment of your dream surprised you?

- How has God used your dream to fulfill His dream of bringing others to Himself?

- How is God currently using you as an ambassador and a minister of reconciliation?

- Who is God telling you to love and forgive? How can you demonstrate God's love to them?

- How can you display humility, gentleness, and patience while bearing with others in love? (see Ephesians 4:2)

- Which of the qualities called for in Colossians 3:12-13 (compassion, kindness, humility, gentleness, patience, forgiveness, and love) do you most readily possess?

- Which ones do you need to cultivate?

Chapter 14
The Dream Expands

Joseph lived in Egypt for many years, where he started his own family with a wife and two boys. We've seen him reach his dream because he faithfully served God regardless of the position God placed him in. He served Pharoah and the Egyptians well by storing up grain for the years of famine. How could he have known his original God-given dream would involve so many people? In this chapter, we will see him reunited with his birth family and continue to live the expanded dream God gave him.

As we continue to serve God faithfully in all areas, we are likely to see our dreams expand. We may start with a small local ministry and see it go global. Or we may minister to a few and see God bring us many more to bless. Regardless of how many people we reach, we are to focus on doing the work God assigns. As people living in the twenty-first century, we think in terms of numbers, but the accurate measure of faithful ministry is obedience. We are to obey God in whatever He says and trust Him to bless however many He chooses.

I have seen God expand my dream—from initially teaching a small class in my church to teaching at other churches and special events. He has allowed me to join an already established ministry and teach at monthly events and a yearly conference. Through this, I have connected with and been able to serve many new people. Many have read articles I have written for an online magazine, and now I am writing this book to help others discover and live their God-given dreams.

Joseph's family prepared to move. Jacob and his family placed all their possessions on the carts Joseph provided and headed to Egypt. When they stopped at Beersheba, Jacob offered sacrifices to God, and God spoke to him in a vision, saying,

> "Jacob! Jacob! ... I am God, the God of your father ... Do not be afraid to go down to Egypt, for I will make you into a great nation there. I will go down to Egypt with you, and I will surely bring you back again. And Joseph's own hand will close your eyes" ... Jacob brought with him to Egypt his sons and grandsons and his daughters and granddaughters—all his offspring. (Genesis 46:2-7)

God speaking to Jacob about his family moving to Egypt reminds us all our dreams are a part of God's plan for the world. Jacob's dream didn't begin with him. The dream began with the promise God gave Abram. God called him and promised, "I will make you into a great nation, and I will bless you" (Genesis 12:2). Later, God changed his name to Abraham and repeated the promise (Genesis 17:5-6) and informed him the promise would come through his son, Isaac (Genesis 17:21).

God then spoke the promise directly to Isaac in saying,

> For to you and your descendants I will give all these lands and will confirm the oath I swore to your father Abraham. I will make your descendants as numerous as the stars in the sky and will give them

all these lands, and through your offspring all nations on earth will be blessed. (Genesis 26:3-4)

Then He spoke the same promise to Jacob saying,

> I am the Lord, the God of your father Abraham and the God of Isaac. I will give you and your descendants the land on which you are lying. Your descendants will be like the dust of the earth ... All peoples on earth will be blessed through you and your offspring. I am with you and will watch over you wherever you go, and I will bring you back to this land. I will not leave you until I have done what I have promised you. (Genesis 28:13-15)

Finally, God assured Jacob and reminded him of the promise as he headed to Egypt,

"Do not be afraid to go down to Egypt, for I will make you into a great nation there. I will go down to Egypt with you, and I will surely bring you back again" (Genesis 46:3-4).

Do you see how the promise became a collective dream? God determined to use Abraham to make a nation through whom the Savior would come (Genesis 22:18, Galatians 3:16-25). God continued this plan through the family—from Abraham to Isaac to Jacob (also named Israel) to Joseph and his brothers. Jacob needed not be afraid, because God does all He says He will do. He promised to make a great nation, and a great nation He would make.

This is true for us as well—whatever God determines to do through us, He will do. We do not have to be afraid but can walk confidently with God, trusting Him to fulfill the portion of the dream

He entrusts to us. Each of our God-given dreams serve as a part of the plan God has to draw people to Himself and make them His family.

When we struggle to believe God will fulfill and expand our dreams, we can encourage ourselves by remembering what He did through Joseph's family. God worked in their lives to do exactly what He promised He would do.

Sixty-six direct descendants of Jacob went to Egypt with Jacob. As they approached Egypt, Jacob sent Judah ahead to get directions to Goshen. When they arrived, Joseph came in his chariot to meet his father. As soon as Joseph saw Jacob, he ran to him, threw his arms around him, and wept for a long time. Jacob exclaimed with joy, "Now I am ready to die, since I have seen for myself that you are still alive" (Genesis 46:26-30). Jacob felt seeing Joseph again fulfilled his dream. God brought his family to Egypt just as He said He would (Genesis 15:13). But God also planned to give Jacob more time with the son he thought he lost.

Anytime we feel something good is taken from us, we can trust God. Either it was not what was best for us, or He will restore it to us when He is ready. In Joel 2:25 God declares, "I will repay you for the years the locusts have eaten." The locusts in this verse refer directly to the loss the people in the days of Joel's prophecy experienced because of God's judgement. But in looking at God's character, we can trust He restores to us losses we suffer for other reasons. Whether we suffer job loss, the ending of relationships, natural disasters, persecution, or punishment, our God can restore to us anything He determines. We can trust God to provide what we need.

Certainly, we can trust God with our dreams, since they are His dreams. He gives them to us to include us in what He is doing. God places us exactly where He wants us to be so we can do what He calls us to do.

God determined I would be born and raised in a small town in the South. I remained in the same town to raise my family. God has placed me in several churches throughout my adult life and used me in each of them. Having been born in the 1970s, I've lived through the inventions of the internet and mobile phones. I've learned to adapt to the world and its changes so I can minister effectively. God has taught me to see chance meetings as divine appointments and opportunities to share Him with others. I've learned to be content in my circumstances, be flexible, and continue learning so I can help others learn to live their dreams.

God determines our dreams and places us when and where He wants us to fulfill them. We can learn to look for opportunities in all He allows. Any position He gives us is a position He will use to advance His will to those around us.

God placed Jacob, Joseph, and all their family where they needed to be to accomplish His will through them. God raised Joseph to second in position in Egypt to fulfill His word of them sojourning in a foreign land. Joseph presented five of his brothers to Pharaoh. Pharaoh asked the brothers about their occupations. They told him they were shepherds and explained they came to live in Egypt near Joseph until the famine subsided. They reported the famine was severe in Canaan, leaving them nowhere to pasture their flocks, and they requested permission to settle in Goshen (Genesis 47:1-4).

Pharaoh granted permission and requested Joseph put any of the brothers skilled in shepherding in charge of his livestock. Joseph then presented his father Jacob to Pharaoh. When Jacob blessed him, Pharaoh inquired how old he was. Jacob told him he was a hundred and thirty years-old but said his "years have been few and difficult" (Genesis 47:5-10).

What an understatement. Jacob's years had certainly been difficult. Having worked seven years for the love of his life, he received her sister on his wedding night. Then he agreed to seven more years of service to receive his beloved (Genesis 29:27). He watched as his wives quarreled over having children and then suffered the loss of his beloved Rachel at the birth of Benjamin (Genesis 35:16-18). His oldest sons hated his favored son, Joseph, sold him into slavery, and lied to Jacob about it claiming Joseph had been killed by a wild animal (Genesis 37:31-33). He held his grief for over twenty years and now needed to move to a foreign land to escape famine at the age of a hundred and thirty. But all the while, God was faithful.

Dear friend, we may experience heartache and sorrow along our dream paths, but our God is faithful. Whether circumstances in our lives are good or bad, our God is good. Difficult times may tempt us to question His goodness, but He is good. He can't be anything other than good.

In my life, I've experienced heartache. I've lost loved ones to death and seen others walking far from God, making a mess of their lives. In one particularly harsh season, I remember telling God, "I don't understand why You don't fix it." I kept praying and asking this repeatedly as I wept over the situation. I finally came to the place where I could say, "I don't understand why You do not fix it, but even if You never fix it–You are God, and You are good." To this day the situation remains, but my God is good. He always has been, and He always will be.

God showed His goodness to Jacob through restoring his family and providing for them through the famine. "So Joseph settled his father and his brothers in Egypt and gave them property in the best part of the land, the district of Rameses, as Pharaoh directed. Joseph also provided his father and his brothers and all his father's household with food, according to the number of their children" (Genesis 47:11-12).

Even in Egypt, a foreign pagan land, God provided for and protected Jacob and his family. They were allowed to live in the land of Goshen, in the district of Rameses. As shepherds, which the Egyptians disliked, they lived separately from the Egyptians, ensuring they maintained their identity as a distinct people. But their presence in Egypt partially fulfilled the promise God made to bless all people through their family (Genesis 12:3). Through Joseph, God provided food for the Egyptians and for the entire world. The ultimate fulfillment of Genesis 12:3 would come through Jesus being born into Jacob's family.

God wants to bless the world through us. He wants us to use the dreams He gives us to bless others and lead them to Himself. Through connection with Jesus, His Son, He has called us to Himself as His special people. But like Joseph's family in Egypt, He desires us to live separately from the world as we work to reveal Him to those who live in it.

Jesus prayed for all believers, saying, "I have given them your word and the world has hated them, for they are not of the world any more than I am of the world. My prayer is not that you take them out of the world but that you protect them from the evil one. They are not of the world, even as I am not of it" (John 17:14-16). Jesus was not of this world. He entered the world to bring God's word and fulfill His mission of reconciliation, but He did not become a part of the world. He lived in perfect righteousness, glorifying the Father in all He did.

Now, God calls us to do the same. Jesus has given us the word, and we are to spread it even if the world hates us for it. We are to be in the world but not of the world, meaning we minister to those in the world, but we do not conform to the world's ways. As we live our God-given dreams for Him, He will protect us from evil and accomplish all He desires to accomplish through us, just as He did with Joseph and his family.

God blessed the entire world through Joseph and the provision he made during the years of famine. And God blessed Pharaoh through Joseph's leadership by making him rich despite the famine. The people of Egypt bought food from the storehouses that Joseph had created, until all their money was spent. Then Joseph began exchanging their livestock for grain. He collected all the horses, sheep, goats, cattle, and donkeys from the people. When all the money and livestock were gone, the people came to Joseph, saying they had nothing left except their bodies and their land. Joseph agreed to take their land and make them servants of Pharaoh. In this way, everything in Egypt, including the people, became Pharaoh's possessions. Joseph established a system where the people would farm the land for Pharaoh and give him a fifth of all the land's produce (Genesis 47:13-26). Again, we see God causing Joseph's earthly master to prosper because of his faithfulness. Through Joseph, Pharaoh became rich. But God richly blessed Joseph by bringing his family back together. As God continued His plan for Joseph's family one step at a time, He will lead us through the fulfillment of our dreams.

God will continue to use, grow, and guide us as we follow Him along our dream paths. He will greatly bless the world around us as we fulfill our God-given dreams, and He will use us to keep advancing His vision of bringing others to Himself. Keep moving forward, dreamer, as God expands your dreams and multiplies them to further His kingdom.

Dream Notes:

- All our dreams are a part of the master plan God has for the world to draw people to Himself as a family.
- The accurate measure of faithful ministry is obedience.
- We are to obey God in whatever He says and trust Him to bless however many He chooses.
- God will fulfill the portion of the dream He entrusts to us.
- God will provide what we need and restore the losses we experience on our dream paths, if we need them.
- God will use every position in which He places us to advance His dream.
- We may experience heartache and sorrow along our dream paths, but our God is good and faithful.

- God wants us to use our God-given dreams to bless others and bring them to Him.
- God will continue to use, grow, and guide us as we follow Him down our dream paths.
- As we continue forward with our dreams, God will expand and multiply them to advance His kingdom.

Dream Work:

- How has God expanded your dream?
- Make a list of the steps God has led you through as you have learned to walk your dream path.
- What major life changes have you experienced on your path? How has this affected the living of your dream?
- Have your years seemed difficult? If so, what did God teach you through the difficulties?
- What losses have you experienced? Have you seen God restore to you what you lost?
- How can you remind yourself of the goodness of God when times seem dark?
- How has God provided for you through the years?
- How can you focus on bringing others to Him as you live your part of the dream?

Chapter 15
Dreams Live On

Today, we will say goodbye to Jacob and all his sons, including Joseph. We journeyed with Joseph and watched as God fulfilled the dreams He gave him. I pray you have discovered your dream and found instruction and encouragement to live it out in the land God has given you. As God blessed Jacob, his family, Egypt, and all the lands through Joseph, may He bless everyone you encounter along your dream path.

As we saw in the last chapter, the Israelites (Joseph's family) settled in Egypt in the region of Goshen. While living there, they acquired property and their numbers grew. Jacob lived in Egypt for seventeen years until the age of one hundred and forty-seven. When Jacob realized he was nearing death, he called for Joseph and had him promise to bury him in Canaan with his ancestors (Genesis 47:27-31).

Joseph then brought his sons Manasseh and Ephraim to Jacob, who rejoiced, saying to Joseph, "I never expected to see your face again, and now God has allowed me to see your children too" (Genesis 48:11). He then blessed Joseph through Ephraim and Manasseh saying, "May the God before whom my fathers Abraham and Isaac walked faithfully, the God who has been my shepherd all my life to this day, the Angel who has delivered me from all harm—may he bless these boys. May they be called by my name and the names of my fathers Abraham and Isaac, and may they increase greatly on the earth." Through this, Jacob counted Manasseh and Ephraim as his sons, resulting in Joseph receiving a double portion of the inheritance (Genesis 48:15-16).

God gave Jacob seventeen years with his son Joseph in Egypt and allowed him to meet his grandsons. God restored what Jacob had lost and provided for him and his family during the famine by bringing him to Egypt. But Egypt was not his home, and he longed to be buried with his ancestors in his homeland.

As we pursue our dreams by serving God, it's wise to remember that Earth is not our true home. Just as God promised Jacob's family the land of Canaan, He has also promised us a better homeland in the future. Peter refers to Christians as "foreigners and exiles" because we do not belong to this world (1 Peter 2:11). We have already seen how Jesus prayed for us to be in the world but not of this world (John 17:14-16). And He promised He will come back for us— "My Father's house has many rooms; if that were not so, would I have told you that I am going there to prepare a place for you? And if I go and prepare a place for you, I will come back and take you to be with me that you also may be where I am" (John 14:2-3).

Knowing Jesus is preparing a place for us to live with Him in the future, so we serve Him now. We believe He is coming again to take us to our future home, "For here we do not have an enduring city, but we are looking for the city that is to come" (Hebrews 13:14). In that city, we will receive all the blessings God desires to give us and rewards for the work we have done here, but the greatest blessing is being with our Lord Jesus forever.

Before Jacob died, he spoke a blessing over each of his sons, prophesying about the contribution each would make as a future leader of the tribe of Israel (Genesis 49). Using the terminology in this book, he spoke according to the dream God placed on each son and his descendants. At the end of Jacob's blessing, Genesis 49:28 declares, "All these are the twelve tribes of Israel, and this is what their father says to them when he blessed them, giving each the blessing appropriate to him." This reminds us that we each play our individual role in the grand dream God has for the earth. God grants us the blessings appropriate to our dreams. He equips us and gives us the strength to fulfill the part of the dream required for each day. It is our responsibility to live the dream He gives us, as it was with each of Jacob's sons.

"When Jacob had finished giving instructions to his sons, he drew his feet up into the bed, breathed his last and was gathered to his people" (Genesis 49:33). Joseph mourned for his father and instructed the physicians of Egypt to embalm him, which took forty days. After they mourned Jacob for seventy days, Joseph, his brothers, and many Egyptians took Jacob's body and buried it in the land of Canaan. "So Jacob's sons did as he had commanded them: They carried him to the land of Canaan and buried him in the cave ... which Abraham had bought along with the field as a burial place from Ephron the Hittite" (Genesis 50:1-13).

Jacob finished his earthly dream, but his dream lived on in his sons. As we discussed previously, God was making Himself a nation through Jacob's family. This promise started with Jacob's grandfather,

Abraham, and it would continue throughout the ages. It was now Joseph and his brothers' turn to carry on the dream.

After returning from burying their father, Joseph's brothers feared Joseph might now seek revenge for the wrongs they had done to him as a child. So, they sent word to Joseph, saying, "Your father left these instructions before he died: 'This is what you are to say to Joseph: I ask you to forgive your brothers for the sins and the wrongs they committed in treating you so badly.' Now please forgive the sins of the servants of the God of your father." When Joseph heard this message, he burst into tears. His brothers came and bowed down before Joseph, saying, "We are your slaves" (Genesis 50:14-18). But Joseph reassured them and spoke kindly to them. "Don't be afraid. Am I in the place of God? You intended to harm me, but God intended it for good to accomplish what is now being done, the saving of many lives. So then, don't be afraid. I will provide for you and your children" (Genesis 50:19-21). Joseph again extended forgiveness to his brothers. He recognized God was the one who brought him to Egypt and explained God used the harm they intended him for good.

As we live our dream, we need not fear man. We can trust God to work all things out for our good and according to His purpose. As we trust Him, we can serve Him faithfully without worrying about what others might do to us. Matthew 10:28 instructs, "Do not be afraid of those who kill the body but cannot kill the soul." The Apostle Paul is an excellent example of this. He focused on pleasing God without worrying about what others thought or did. He said, "Am I now trying to win the approval of human beings, or of God? Or am I trying to please people? If I were still trying to please people, I would not be a servant of Christ" (Galatians 1:10). God calls us as servants to obey and please Him in all we do. As we focus on Him, follow His lead, and fulfill His tasks, we will complete the work He has for us. When we have done the will of God, we will receive what He has promised (Hebrews 10:36).

Joseph and his entire family stayed in Egypt, where they had many descendants. As Joseph neared death, he reminded his family that God would fulfill His promise by bringing them out of Egypt and returning them to the land He promised to Abraham. Joseph made them promise to take his bones with them when God led them back to the land of Canaan. "So Joseph died at the age of a hundred and ten. And after they embalmed him, he was placed in a coffin in Egypt" (Genesis 50:22-26).

Years later, God would deliver the children of Israel (Joseph's family) from Egypt with a great deliverance. "These are the names of the sons of Israel who went to Egypt with Jacob, each with his family: Reuben, Simeon, Levi and Judah; Issachar, Zebulun and Benjamin; Dan and Naphtali; Gad and Asher. The descendants of Jacob numbered seventy in all; Joseph was already in Egypt." Joseph, his brothers, and all their generation died, but the Israelites remained in Egypt and multiplied and filled the land (Exodus 1:1-7). Thus, fulfilling the promise made to their ancestor Abraham (Genesis 15:5, 22:17).

Four hundred and thirty years after coming to Egypt, the Israelites exited with as many as two million people (six hundred thousand men plus women and children). They brought out much livestock and many possessions they gained from the Egyptians (Exodus 12:35-40).

"Moses took the bones of Joseph with him because Joseph had made the Israelites swear an oath. He had said, 'God will surely come to your aid, and then you must carry my bones up with you from this place'" (Exodus 13:19). Years later, when Israel returned and conquered the land of Canaan which was given to them by God, they buried Joseph's bones on land Jacob bought and gave this portion of the land to Joseph's descendants as an inheritance (Joshua 24:32).

Joseph and all his contemporaries died, but the dream lived on because it was God's dream. He worked all things according to His plan to make a nation from Abraham and ultimately bring His Son into the world through them.

Much later in Israel's history, God promised through the prophet Hosea He would call a people to Himself who were not His people. "Yet the Israelites will be like the sand on the seashore, which cannot be measured or counted. In the place where it was said to them, 'You are not my people,' they will be called 'children of the living God'" (Hosea 1:10). "I will plant her for myself in the land; I will show my love to the one I called 'Not my loved one.' I will say to those called 'Not my people'; 'You are my people'; and they will say, 'You are my God'" (Hosea 2:23).

We who believe in God through Jesus are the ones who have done so. Although we were not born into the family of Abraham, we have been chosen by God to be His people. Now, it is our turn to call all people to Him. By living out the dreams He gives us, we can inspire others to come to Him, accept His salvation, and join His family.

Throughout this book, we have used the term "dream" to refer to the desires we feel to work for God. We discussed that God has a plan for all His creation, which is to bring many to Him through His Son and make them His family. Our service to Him is just a small part of a larger dream He works to fulfill.

We observed Joseph and his family's role in the dream and used them as an example to inspire us to remain faithful in our part. I pray you have identified your assignment in the dream and are living it faithfully. May God bless you as He blessed Joseph in everything you do, and may He grant you favor with those around you. May you be the blessing He desires for all you serve.

God is the Dream-giver. He loves us dearly and has chosen us to be a part of His family and His mission. You could say we are His dream. He created us to live the dream He gives us. He designed each of us physically and gave us our unique personalities. We are all "fearfully and wonderfully made" (Psalm 139:14). The Holy Spirit shapes us through the lessons He allows and transforms us into the image of His Son. God determines when and where we live so that we can use our dreams to accomplish what He wants through us.

God is our Dream-giver, who gives each one of us dreams and directs us toward them. He created us for His purpose and gives us desires to achieve His plans. "For we are God's handiwork, created in Christ Jesus to do good works, which God prepared in advance for us to do" (Ephesians 2:10). God saved us through Jesus, took us as His children, and clothed us in righteousness to prepare us for our dreams. His Holy Spirit continues to work in us—purifying, equipping, and preparing us to live our dreams. All circumstances in life strengthen and prepare us to live our God-given dreams. God sparks dreams in us, paralleling His plans for us, and propels us toward our mission.

All the plans God has for His children are good. "'For I know the plans I have for you,' declares the Lord, 'plans to prosper you and not to harm you, plans to give you hope and a future'" (Jeremiah 29:11). We can trust the plan because it is God's plan. He chooses the dreams we receive, and He ensures we fulfill them. God will give us all the time, energy, and skills we need to do whatever He leads us to do. As we faithfully obey Him, He fulfills His mission and makes our dreams become realities. "He gives us the victory through our Lord Jesus Christ" (1 Corinthians 15:57). Even if we don't have a clear sense of the dreams God has planned for us, we can serve Him, trusting He is working His plan. As we live our lives for Him, we will discover the dreams God has for us.

Life is God's dream. Our dreams include far more than we can imagine. Our God-given dreams, big and small, work together to fulfill God's ultimate plan of drawing people to Himself as a family through salvation. Having created us for relationship and fellowship, He calls us to help others come to Him. We participate in His dream by sharing Jesus with others.

God calls us to use our dreams to minister to others, expand the kingdom, and draw others closer to Him. Every step toward our dreams is an opportunity to bless someone and introduce them to Jesus. As we live our dreams, we help others and glorify God.

Our dreams might not look exactly as we imagined, but they will align perfectly with what God has planned. Although our path to those dreams may not be easy, we can trust our Dream-giver to guide us toward them. God fulfills His promises in His perfect timing and way. Living each day as if it were our current dream pushes us closer to the realization of our God-given dreams. We can serve God faithfully, knowing that He controls how our dreams are interpreted and fulfilled. God never forgets us or our dreams. He will complete His purpose through us as we walk down the dream path one day at a time.

God acts as our Dream-leader as He leads us down the path to our dreams. Knowing He controls the plan and enables us to reach the dream helps us walk confidently down our dream paths. Any delay or obstacle we face has been carefully designed by God to strengthen us and prepare us for our dreams. Dream work may be hard work, but we can do it. God works for us and in us. He supplies whatever we need for our dreams to come true. "For the eyes of the LORD range throughout the earth to strengthen those whose hearts are fully committed to him" (2 Chronicles 16:9). He will fulfill the portion of the dream He entrusts to us as we obey Him.

We live the dream as we give each day to God and strive to please Him. Living for God is less about the dream and more about glorifying Him. Every opportunity He provides is an opportunity to know Him better and reveal Him to others. Our ultimate good work is to glorify God by faithfully serving Him in our dreams. We please Him as we obey and trust Him to bless whomever He chooses.

God is our Dream-giver, Dream-leader, and Dream-fulfiller. We can trust Him to reveal and fulfill our dreams as we serve Him faithfully throughout our lives. Our mission isn't complete until we reach heaven. As we live for Him, each day by doing the work He assigns us, we will live our dreams and see His come true. He will be pleased with our lives. When our part of the mission is complete, we will be gathered to our heavenly homeland and hear Him say, "Well done, good and faithful servant! ... Come and share your master's happiness!" (Matthew 25:21).

We can trust God to fulfill every promise in His Word and to empower us to fulfill the plans He has for us. In giving us dreams, He ensures their realization. As we obey Him, keep walking down our dream paths, and give Him all the glory, we will see the fulfillment of His dream in our lives. Let's keep advancing as God expands our dreams and multiplies them to advance His kingdom. He will fulfill the dream. "The one who calls you is faithful, and he will do it" (1 Thessalonians 5:24).

Dream Notes:

- God is the Dream-giver, Dream-leader, and Dream-fulfiller.
- He has given us a specific amount of time on the earth to live our dreams.
- We live our dreams and participate in His, as we complete the tasks, He assigns us.
- The ultimate dream is being in heaven with God.
- Our work here is to help others join His family and prepare to meet Him.
- We can bravely fulfill our mission trusting God to work all things out for our good and according to His purpose.
- Even when we die, the dream lives on.
- We are a small part of the big dream God is fulfilling.
- He will complete His dream for all the earth.

Dream Work:

- Write a purpose statement in your dream journal, clearly stating your dream.

- Outline the steps required to fulfill your dream. Pray over them, and revise as God leads.

- What's the next step on your dream path? How will you step forward with it?

- If you still struggle to recognize your God-given dream, write a prayer that includes questions about His purpose for you.

- Commit to following the leading He gives you. Remember, we often discover our dreams as we live each day serving the Dream-giver.

- Begin a new section in your journal entitled Dream Moments, where you will record how you see God working in your life toward the fulfillment of your dream.

Acknowledgements

I am first and foremost thankful to God my Father, Jesus my Savior, and the Holy Spirit my Guide, who have called me to be Theirs. They loved me, chose me, and invited me to live life with and for Them. They gave me the opportunity to live my God-given Dream of helping others know Them.

To my husband, Clay, who has walked this dream path with me for thirty-five years. Thank you for supporting me and making it possible for me to live my dream. To all my kids and grandkids, I love you. Thank you for loving me in return as Mama and MeeMa.

Thank you to all my friends who have walked through life with me, and my church family who have encouraged me and allowed me to share my spiritual gift with you.

A special thank you to Billie Corley for inviting me to teach alongside her, encouraging me, and mentoring me in women's ministry. To Beebe and Katy Kauffman, who have poured into my writing with teaching, training, and opportunities. To Dorothy Deming, for always reminding me that God would use me, for brainstorming, editing, and re-editing with me to help my writing shine. To Michael Perri, for teaching our class so I could focus on writing, and for all that you have taught me from the Word in the last few years. To Layne Bridges, who read chapter by chapter, giving critique and encouragement. To Cadie Ball and Ben Corley, who read the final manuscript and provided valuable feedback and final touches.

Katherine Hutchinson-Hayes, thank you for making my dream happen. Your cheerleading, coaching, advice, editing, friendship, and so much more. Thank you for being true to your God-given dream and allowing me to participate in it.

Thank you, Pastor Brian Jones, for teaching the truth of God's word faithfully. Thank you for keeping me focused on God and His Word, and for encouraging me that the message of my book is important to God's family.

Karen Griffin is a Word-filled teacher, author, and speaker. She currently serves with Billie Corley Ministries where she teaches at monthly Bible studies and an annual fall retreat. In her church, she serves as adult Sunday school teacher and women's ministry leader. She has articles published in several compilations published by Light House Bible Studies and is a regular contributor to their online magazine, Refresh.

She speaks at women's events where she challenges women to dig deep into God's Word. Her passion and love for Jesus is evident as she lifts Him up to be admired and adored. As she dissects and explains Bible passages, she challenges listeners to understand and apply them to their lives. Karen encourages others to be rooted in the truth of God's word and living according to the purpose He has given them.

Karen has a B.S. in psychology and has studied God's Word in depth for over thirty years. While her greatest passion is Bible study, she also enjoys flower gardening, boating with her husband, and playing games with her friends.

She regards her most important ministry to be that of being wife to her husband Clay, mother to three grown children and two sons-in-law, and MeeMa to four grandsons. She is a life-time resident of Tifton, GA.

Connect with Karen:

Facebook: @KarenGibbsGriffin
Blog: www.karengriffin.blog

Coming 2026:

Light for Clouded Eyes: Seeing Life Clearly Through the Lens of Scripture